Author of:

Ageless Wisdom

The Gamer

The Power of Optimism

Destined for Greatness

The Triumph of the Spirit

Oh Yes We Can!

Piggy Bank Basics

Dare to Be a Millionaire

Dare to Be a Millionaire Workbook

Dare to Be a Millionaire Quotes

The Power of Money

Dreamers and Doers

GREATNESS AWAITS

Putting Your Dreams into Action

Dr. Robert L. Lawson

BALBOA
PRESS
A DIVISION OF HAY HOUSE

Balboa Press books may be ordered through booksellers or by contacting:

Balboa Press
A Division of Hay House
1663 Liberty Drive
Bloomington, IN 47403
www.balboapress.com
1 (877) 407-4847

Because of the dynamic nature of the Internet, any web addresses or links contained in this book may have changed since publication and may no longer be valid. The views expressed in this work are solely those of the author and do not necessarily reflect the views of the publisher, and the publisher hereby disclaims any responsibility for them.

The author of this book does not dispense medical advice or prescribe the use of any technique as a form of treatment for physical, emotional, or medical problems without the advice of a physician, either directly or indirectly. The intent of the author is only to offer information of a general nature to help you in your quest for emotional and spiritual well-being. In the event you use any of the information in this book for yourself, which is your constitutional right, the author and the publisher assume no responsibility for your actions.

Any people depicted in stock imagery provided by Thinkstock are models, and such images are being used for illustrative purposes only.
Certain stock imagery © Thinkstock.

Print information available on the last page.

ISBN: 978-1-5043-8906-8 (sc)
ISBN: 978-1-5043-8905-1 (hc)
ISBN: 978-1-5043-8907-5 (e)

Library of Congress Control Number: 2017914619

Balboa Press rev. date: 10/17/2017

Dedicated to my wife,

Dr. Shannon L. Lawson;

My mom,

Mary Irene Payne;

My aunt,

Nora Faye Lawson;

My grandmother,

Ethel Wilson Lawson;

My uncle,

Hollis Thomas Lawson;

My grandfather,

Robert Henry Lawson;

My three sons,

Robert Leon Lawson Jr.,

James Allen Lawson,

Michael Emerson Lawson.

I love you all dearly.

To: Harvey Alston —

Be the Best!

Contents *Doc*

Book II

Acknowledgments

I am especially grateful to these individuals, who have served as mentors, colleagues, friends and sources of inspiration. Holly Woodruff, Matt Cameron, Mike Fadeley, Heather Bertram, Andrea Faulkner, Chad McKibben, Thad Wallace, John Copas, Mike Jennings, Jim Garrett, Tina Hoskey, Kristin Depenbrock, Perianne Germann, Jerry Underwood, Gar Siegla, Michael Smith, Christy Lucas, Vern Hawkins, Tom Ramey, Christopher Burrows, Jon Saxton, Debbie Bettendorf, Dr. Jeffrey Fisher, Dustin Weaver, Zach Graves, Dan Staggs, Steve Mullins, Tracee Garrett, Mark Anthony Garrett, Chris Baird, Deanna Blanton, Geoffrey Smith, Will Vickery, Barb Coulter, Nancy Thornsberry, Gene Murphy, Robin Murphy, Tony Murphy, Richard Holt, Coleen Kosan, Holli Pellman, Darian Pellman, Frank Beach, Dr. Phil Woolf, Ralph Kraus, Dr. F. David Wilkin, Ray Ellis, Chuck Whaley, James Carter, Dr. Velta Kelley, Dean Rinehart, Dr. Janice Mercier Wade, Dr. Clyde Evans, Arthur Lanham, Dr. Joan Adkins, Dr. Marvin O. Mitchell, Dr. Peter Mills, Paul Lloyd, Aleta Mays Polley, Harvey Alston, Toni Alston, Dennis Fravel, Shawn Tomlin, Kelly Tomlin, Melissa Cropper, Bernie Cropper, Susan Noll, Robin Swartz, Brad Fitzpatrick, Dee Dee Faust, Brenda Dixon, Brent Caldwell, Jamie Louden, Joyce Smith, Donna Devries, Ralph Sininger, Keith McGuire, Brent Saunders, Rosemary Evans, Nancy Evans, Sarah Evans-Moore, Margaret Evans, Leesa McGuire, Mike Frank, Tyson Murphy, Cace Murphy, Chloe Murphy, Bob Sims, Paul Kuhn, Dr. Paul Hines, Steve Roese, Don Staggs, Ella Coleman, Willie Johnson, Willie

Jolley, Semia Bray, Ilinda Reese, Lucius Lewis, Patricia Wingard Carson, Harvey Alston, Henry Ford, Beverly Crabtree, Susan Haft, Sandy Petrie-Forgey, Margaret Bernstein, Tara Nicely and Barbara Reynolds, Wanda, I. Colon Mollfulleda, Kim Riley, Sandy Kellam, Jessica Orr, Brady Womack, Clarence Parker, Patricia Parker, Richard Jordan, Teresa Stockton, Jackie King, Obadiah Harris, Elsie Harris-Shabazz, and so many more.

I am also especially grateful to all of my former students and colleagues at the University of Rio Grande, Gallia Academy High School, Marshall University, Ohio University, Shawnee State University, Georgetown Exempted Village Schools, and my current and former Chillicothe High School students in Chillicothe, Ohio.

I would never have accomplished this without the incredible inspirational writings and speeches of such noteworthy individuals as Ralph Waldo Emerson, Henry David Thoreau, Williams James Tilley, Zig Ziglar, Tom Ziglar, Helen Keller, Dr. John Maxwell, Dr. Robert Schuller, Napoleon Hill, Dr. Stephen Covey, Dr. Wayne Dyer, Anthony Robbins, Brian Tracy, James Allen, Les Brown, Dr. David Schwartz, Dr. Dean Keith Simonton, and numerous other speakers and writers. These individuals have helped me to learn that there are no limitations to what the human spirit can achieve because of its incredible and unrelenting persistence and resilience.

Finally, what really puts one over the top are the incredible, inspirational, and dedicated individuals like Louise Hay, who founded Hay House Publishing. I am so grateful and thankful to have the opportunity to work with such professional representatives at Balboa Press, a subsidiary of Hay House—people like Lisa Vyas, my publishing consultant; Mary Oxley, my publishing associate; and a host of other experts who are helping me to position my manuscript in the best possible way to secure the maximum results afforded to me through the publishing industry.

I am so grateful for this magnificent assistance afforded me and deeply humbled by this amazing and incredible experience. I want to take this opportunity to say thanks to each and every one of you from the bottom of my heart for your professional assistance and guidance through this extraordinary process. This is an unequaled privilege. I especially want to thank Mark Anthony Garrett and Tracee Garrett. Tracee has worked tirelessly in helping me to get this manuscript ready for submission to Balboa Press.

*The divine deposit of destiny that God has placed in
your heart cannot be stopped by anyone.*
—Dr. Robert L. Lawson

Dreams without plans are merely wishes.
—Dr. Robert L. Lawson

*Success happens when thousands of hours of preparation
meet one moment of opportunity.*
—Anonymous

*Authors by the hundreds can tell you stories by the thousands
of those rejection slips before they found a publisher
who was willing to gamble on an unknown.*
—Zig Ziglar

Greatness Awaits

Greatness awaits those who strive for the best.
The moment you truly believe,
If you give of yourself 100 percent,
There's nothing you cannot achieve.

If you put in the work that's required of you,
And you push yourself clear to the max,
You'll dine with true royalty day after day—
And these are just simply the facts.

Life is unfolding each moment for you,
And right now, you're still in control.
If you simply refuse to give up on your dream,
It's a fact you'll accomplish your goal.

Work is the secret to massive success;
It's the royal path to the top.
No matter how curvy or windy the road,
You must stay the course and not stop.

Greatness awaits at the top of the mountain,
As you seek for the treasures beyond.
What lies at the tip of your outstretched hand
Is the hope that remains with each dawn.

Achievement

Achievement is our greatest goal,
So set your standards high,
And don't suppress your strong desires
Until you've reached the sky.

Your heart, my heart, and every heart
Upon this world combined—
Is useless when it's not unfurled
Before the end of time.

It's what you are inside of you;
You must yourself express,
Instead of bottling up your cares
And keeping them suppressed.

Our job is helping everyone
To find a purpose here.
It is the greatest thing to do:
Be more than just sincere.

My hope is built on nothing less:
A strong desire, a will of bliss.
And I wish to each of you,
Pure joy and happiness.

Few know of life's beginnings.
Men behold the goal achieved.
The warrior, when his sword flashes
Red triumph in the noonday sun.
The poet, when his lyre hangs on the palm.
The statesman, when the crowd proclaim his voice
And mould opinion on his gifted tongue.

They count not life's first steps
And never think upon the many miserable hours,
When hope deferred was sickness to the heart.
They reckon not the battle and the march,
Long privations of a wasted youth.
They never see the banner till unfurled.

What are to them the solitary nights,
Passed pale and anxious by the sickly lamp,
Till the young poet wins the world at last
To listen to the music long his own?

The crowds attend the statesman's fiery mind,
But they do not trace its struggle
Or its long expectancy.
Hard are life's early steps,
And but that youth is buoyant, confident,
And strong in hope,
Men would behold its threshold and despair.

By: Landon

"Take the chains off your mind and think in a way you've never even thought before. Start doing like you've never done before, and refuse to allow the negativity and the manipulation of others to prevent you from moving forward. This mindset that is designed to fuel your imagination and creativity will enable you to break through manmade barriers that were designed to stifle your growth. This new attitude about life will take you to places you never dreamed possible. Do it meticulously one step at a time, and you will arrive at your designated destination."

True Greatness

A power outside of time itself,
Seeking to answer your call,
Stands at the door of conviction
As the wisdom encompassing all.

This illimitable measure of truth,
Determined to aid in your quest,
Takes flight with the wings of direction
When you destine yourself for the best.

The consistent approach used in winning,
As you climb toward your ultimate high,
Is the key to the struggle's beginning
As you challenge and reach for the sky.

As you move with a definite purpose
And you seek to maintain your desire;
Be fierce and truly relentless;
Heap coals on your internal fire.

For those who inspire true greatness
Are blessed and most apt to receive.
But the question that each one must answer
Is "How strongly do you truly believe?"

Introduction

Greatness is an abstract concept that is somewhat difficult for many to define and comprehend, yet it is easily recognizable when it is observed. It is a quality and a certain disposition that distinguishes one from its contemporaries or sets an individual apart from others.

Most people have the potential to be great, but most never achieve greatness. There are many attributes required for one to achieve a level of greatness. Perhaps this is why it is so difficult to ascertain. To discuss and talk about it is one thing, but to achieve it is entirely another.

Greatness is not a concept for the fainthearted individual or for those individuals who are emotionally insecure. It is not for those individuals who are not willing to make a total commitment to pursue it, or to create a vision or a plan of action that must be executed for its obtainment.

On the contrary, true greatness may very well require years to obtain.

Even then, there are no guarantees that one will ever master its elusive qualities. Yet it is the one thing to which many aspire. Whether it is an incredible athlete who embodies the qualities of greatness, a business guru, a teacher, a television personality, a politician, a scientist, a singer, a motivational speaker, or a service man, you will always know when you are in the presence of greatness.

All of these individuals exude a confidence level and an aura of contagious enthusiasm that makes you feel that you too can become great. Great people not only have and possess the desire to see you maximize your own potential, but they also possess the skill sets, the ideologies, and the mindset that are necessary to help you to cultivate your own potential for greatness to the highest degree possible.

The difference for you lies in how you handle life on a daily basis when you're not in the presence of greatness. Will you still take the time to work toward your goals and dreams on a continual basis? Will you still take the time to develop an action plan and follow through on it? Will you put in the necessary time, energy, and effort on a daily basis to achieve all the goals you have set for yourself?

Will you develop a linear focus toward what needs to be accomplished in your life? Will you stop allowing those negative influences in your life and those negative habits you've developed to stop being the distractions and roadblocks to the kind of life you'd really like to live? When you are able to reach a point in your life when you can be honest with yourself about why you haven't taken the steps necessary to realize your own dreams, that is when your life will begin to assume a more powerful and manifold purpose.

Nothing positive or good can happen until you are willing to take positive steps and consistent action day in and day out as you strive daily to reach the goals and dreams that you have set for yourself. The circumstances in which you currently find yourself, as well as the friends with whom you associate, will be the primary dictators of influence in your life. Your ultimate success requires a deep self-examination and a bold staring of truth in the face. Do you like your current circumstances? Are your current friends interested in seeing you become successful or are they sometimes not accepting of your ambitious nature? Perhaps it's time that you surround yourself with a new set of friends.

If your life is ever going to change, the bottom line is this: you are going to have to be the one to change it. A success-oriented mentality cannot survive or grow in an environment that is fraught with negativity and unbelief. This kind of environment is a graveyard for dreams and goals. Pessimism is a destroyer of life and works hard to cripple and defeat desire, innovation, and creativity. Pessimism hates originality and does what it can to derail the flames of enthusiasm, positivism, and motivation.

Those individuals who dare to be great are completely different from most other individuals who inhabit this planet. For one thing, over the years they have managed to develop strong minds that are not easily swayed by naysayers. They have learned to turn deaf ears to critics and those who are opposed to their way of thinking. That's why they are able to set themselves apart from the masses of individuals who live in total chaos and confusion with little to no direction in life.

When you hear individuals spend all of their time complaining about how other people have it so good and how life is not fair, and they remain intent on giving you a sob story about why their lives are so miserable, this should be a red flag to you that these people have no ambition, no dreams, and no goals. They simply want you to commiserate with them. Misery loves company. Get away from these people fast, or you will die a slow death.

Connect with like-minded individuals who have a desire to make something out of their lives and are in fact willing to work toward the achievement of their lifelong goals and ambitions. After all, life *does* matter, and it's important to help others to realize the qualities for which they should be striving.

Every day you arise, life is all about the choices you make. It's those choices you make every single day that determine your direction in life. Whom you spend time with, where you go, and what you do on a daily basis are the primary motivators and influencers in your life. How are you being influenced? What materials are you reading? What do these materials cause you to think about or do? Why is that? What do you need to change in your life? Why do you need to change that? These are the questions you need to ask yourself on a daily basis.

For those individuals who have the ultimate desire to make major changes in their own lives, as well as in the lives of many others, it requires think time. You have to take time to plan and improvise. Understand that your own original thoughts are extremely powerful and have tremendous merit. In order to achieve true greatness and unbelievable success, it requires a deep-seated belief in yourself, your abilities, and all the talents and skills with which God has endowed you.

One of the greatest cripplers of dreams in our society is that far too many individuals lack self-confidence and don't truly believe in themselves. If they are to ever become successful in life, they must begin changing the internal perception they have of themselves and seeing themselves as they truly are: powerful, successful, tenacious, and relentless beyond measure.

The key is this: whoever you were, you no longer have to be that person. You can become the new you. You are the only one who needs to give yourself permission to do that. Nobody else's opinion of you matters. Your opinion of yourself is the only one that matters. The new you is the person who possesses a greater degree of self-confidence, the person who has now mastered a new skill or a new ability, the person who is better at what he does today than he was yesterday because he has put in the time, energy, and effort to become better—and as a result of that, he *is* better.

What a remarkable transformation that has occurred, and all because you invested the time it takes to become better. It is a thing that can happen to all of us on a daily basis, and the reason why is so very simple:

no matter how good we are at what we do, the more we can learn about our craft, the more new approaches we can use, the more technology we can incorporate, and the more strategies we can implement, the more we can heighten and sharpen the internal awareness we have of ourselves.

A new mentor can emerge to teach us even more about ourselves and our capabilities. The more we can soak in and learn, the better we can become. This is the royal road to greatness. All who possess the internal drive that is insatiable has the opportunity to get there. This is the road we must travel; no other path will get us there. We must go directly through the fire to be tempered and molded so that we can emerge victorious on the other side.

Although it is incredible and powerful to know and to read what others think, what will move you forward the most is what *you* think. It is your ability to take consistent action on the things you know to do that will eventually enable you to rise and grasp the very pinnacle of success. If there is any kind of special secret to success, it's taking positive action on a consistent basis.

You have to feel motivated, and you have to act on that motivation consistently to continue moving forward. This book that you are holding in your hands at this very instant can be the key to your total and complete transformation. It will save you from years of self-imposed captivity by helping you to stay motivated and inspired throughout as you read page after page of transcendent ideas that you can place in action to enable you to become the person you were destined to become as you travel this practical, inspirational, and intellectual road to greatness. You are wished an abundance of success and happiness in your ultimate quest to be one of the very best. Let's get started on this awesome journey right now!

Putting Your Dreams into Action

Action Cures Fear.
—Dr. David Schwartz

Putting your dreams into action requires some incredibly serious decision-making on your part. The more you are able to discover about yourself and the essence of your own capabilities, the more effective you are going to be in setting out to accomplish exactly what it is you intend to do. In fact, the more precise, focused, and accurate you are, the more likely you will be to arrive at your destination.

In William James Tilley's powerful book *Masters of the Situation*, written in 1889, he says, "It is probable that not one individual out of a thousand has an adequate conception for what he is capable of doing. The possibilities that lie before anyone would probably astound him if he knew at any one moment what they were. The latent and undiscovered and undeveloped talent and possibilities are ever before you. Your future ever awaits."

These magnificent words are truly amazing and are pregnant with a myriad of possibilities—and yet so few will take advantage of them as a way of realizing their full potential. Many times the reasons are quite clear; at other times they are not. I have discovered that taking action has so much to do with what you can do with your power in believing in your own abilities, talents, and skills to keep yourself moving forward in life. You can create and complete many of your best achievements by strengthening your belief level in your own capabilities and effectiveness as a person.

One of my most powerful friends and mentors, Dr. Jeffrey Fisher, has been and continues to be a highly influential individual in my life. His ability to make me better at my craft is amazingly impactful.

In order for you to maximize your potential, the one thing you don't need are individuals who constantly tear you down and make you feel worthless. That is the quickest way for your dream to be killed. My advice is to remove yourself from that environment immediately if you can. Now, let's be realistic here. Some individuals in home situations are not even remotely compatible. Sometimes your spouse is inflicting all the damage. My second piece of advice is to find a mentor or friend who believes in you as a human being and can support you in your predicament—someone who has the ability to counterbalance the negativity consuming your life.

Dr. Fisher possesses those characteristics. He fully embraces the Japanese kaizen philosophical approach to teaching, training, and development, which encompasses a constant and never-ending improvement approach to teaching and learning. Each time he walks into my classroom to evaluate me, he comes in with a pure, exact, and constructive eye for what he hopes to see. If he doesn't see it, when we meet for my observation soon after, he immediately tells me not only what my strengths are but also those areas that I must work on to become more effective.

For the past three years, Dr. Fisher has been a major confidence builder for me, and I can assure you that my ability as a classroom instructor has far exceeded my own expectations. It is one thing to criticize an individual and then leave him or her wondering about how to improve. It is quite another thing to sit down and discuss in a clear, pristine, and delineated way how to more effectively engage students in the learning process. Dr. Fisher has mastered the art of doing this. As a result, the majority (if not all) of his instructional personnel are more effective classroom teachers. Not only are they better teachers, but because of the instructional methodologies and specific practices they've placed in effect, there are fewer discipline problems, and overall classrooms are better managed.

The idea of adhering to a set of instructional guidelines and principles with consistency and an intent that incorporates a focus for learning is applicable not only for classroom instruction but for virtually every aspect of a person's life. You simply have to have enough vision to actually see it and specifically apply it to your life.

Here's how that works. If you have a desire to be successful, you must also have a strong desire to be driven on a daily basis. You cannot do things in a sporadic, haphazard manner and expect to accomplish great things. It doesn't work that way. Feedback is essential to knowing how effective your performance is. Dr. Fisher once said something to me that gave my confidence level a huge boost. Right after he observed one of my classes, he made it a point to let me know several areas that needed some refinement. When I shot him a text that said, "I must've had a bad day," he responded immediately. "You could never have a bad day." At that moment, I clearly understood his intent. He was guiding me through a process. He was not concerned with the content of my instruction; he was intent on showing me how I could more effectively deliver the content.

He later informed me that my lessons garnered strong student engagement; that was not an area in which he had concern. What I needed to do was listen to his advice and implement it in order to become

3

more effective. This increased effectiveness would benefit my students, my colleagues, my principal, my superintendent, my school district, and my community. Most important, it would benefit me. What a powerful life lesson—and it's not limited to the classroom but encompasses every aspect of life.

If you can get to the point where you truly understand that your capabilities are unlimited, then you can start putting your dreams into action. Your belief level in yourself must be tenable and without question. You must know that essential feedback is necessary for continued growth and development, and you must continue moving forward and working with a clear, delineated focus on what you desire to achieve. You must do it daily with consistency and be intentional about it. If you do this, your dreams will become more real and achievable than they have ever been before.

Perhaps one other thing should be mentioned here, especially for those individuals who find themselves constantly criticized by others: the remarkable words of Theodore Roosevelt.

> It is not the critic who counts. It is not the man who points out where the strong man stumbled or whether the doer of great deeds could have done them better. The credit belongs to the individual who is actually in the arena, whose face is marred with dust and sweat and blood, who strives valiantly, who errs, who comes up short again and again and again but who while daring greatly, spends himself in a worthy cause so that his place may not be among those cold and timid souls who know neither victory nor defeat.

And always remember the immortal words of William Jennings Bryan: "Destiny is not a matter of chance. It is a matter of choice. It is not a thing to be hoped for. It is a thing to be achieved."

Someone's Child

Making an effort to say and do positive things with
your own child or someone else's is a huge deal.

When God provides you with an opportunity to make a positive difference in someone's life, you should by no means take it for granted. My life has been spent as an instructor and purveyor of knowledge, and I make an effort daily not only to impart knowledge but to create an environment that encourages growth, creativity, opportunity, and discussion.

Our job as educators is to encourage individuals to grow and become independent thinkers in their own rights so that they can further the process by moving forward to pursue their own dreams, passions, desires, and goals. Over the years, I have encountered many young people whom I have had the fortunate pleasure of influencing in a positive way.

I have had so many meaningful, constructive dialogues. I have lifted the spirits of many of my students, and they have lifted mine in turn. As I reflect on various aspects of my life, I see that so many students have been incredible inspirations to me. If it weren't for them, I would have given up the teaching profession a long time ago. Instead, that profession is exactly what David Hasselcorn said it was: "Teaching is the profession that makes all other professions possible."

And so it is, and so it remains. The duty of an instructor who is in a position to shape, mold, and influence the mind of another human being is one of the most powerful duties on earth.

Your mastery of subject matter or knowledge of content, and the conceptual framework or the process in which you deliver it year after year, doesn't simply reflect a remarkable event as it occurs. Each and every year, you have an opportunity to add to your existing knowledge base, encounter new experiences right there in the classroom, and be exposed to new materials that encourage you to try new ideas and approaches to enhance your classroom performance and close the learning gaps between what your students know and what they don't. As you do this, it enables your students to become even more productive citizens because you have helped them to broaden their knowledge base and improve their skill sets. What a powerful gift!

There is no end to growing, teaching, learning, developing, molding, influencing, and refining. All of these processes are continuous. They are powerful and life changing. The thing that keeps you inspired and encouraged is what you see in the eyes of your students on a daily basis. It's that look of gratitude that greets you. It's that look that says, I'm glad you took the time to be here, to share things with us that could make a difference in our lives, to help us to be better, to do better, to learn a new skill, to perfect an old one, to be a better critical thinker, to raise a level of awareness regarding something I've read, to look at things differently than I did before, to realize that I truly do have potential, to be more consistent with my endeavors, to build my confidence. The life skills that you are teaching your students are beneficial to anyone. These are the wow moments for you and for your students. It's literally the juice of life that keeps you going.

Never lose faith in yourself, and just as important, never lose faith in others. Always remember this fact: God placed you specifically where you are for a reason. In fact, he placed you there for numerous reasons. Whether it's the school of life and hard knocks or the traditional brick-and-mortar school, you are there for multiple reasons. For you traditionalists, every year you return to school at the beginning of a new school year, think about that. Whether it's kindergarten, grade school, middle school, high school, the collegiate environment, or the corporate world, you are there for the specific purpose of inspiring others to learn. You are there for the specific purpose of making a difference in the life of someone's child. Honor that gift.

Someone's Child

As I stand before the masses,
My heart is truly blessed.
For God revealed long ago
My mission and my quest.

His spirit was so gentle,
His voice was clear and mild:
Pour into the open mind,
And life of someone's child.

As you walk this awesome journey,
Bestow on them your gift.
Become the wind beneath their wings,
And give them each a lift.

Help each one to understand
The struggle from the start:
The things that matter most in life
Must live inside your heart.

As I survey their eager faces
And ponder all the while,
The thought I most reflect on
Is, This is someone's child.

We have an opportunity
To measure and to mold,
And turn a life begun as dust
Into a strand of gold.

No matter what the courts may say
With briefs or papers filed,
You can always make a difference
In the life of someone's child.

Vision

Those who cherish a beautiful vision, a lofty ideal
in their hearts, will one day realize it.
—James Allen

A vision is a spiritual insight into the potentiality of an individual. As James Allen so eloquently states in his amazing and insightful treatise, *As a Man Thinketh*, "A vision is a promise of what you shall one day become."

As one traverses life, one must realize that the vision an individual has resides in the human heart, waiting dormant to be brought to life. A vision is the illimitable dream of palpable substance. The achievement or the fulfillment of a life vision is indigenous to a life purpose. The two are inextricably linked.

It is exactly as the great Charles Swindoll has said: "A vision is essential for survival. It is spawned by faith, sustained by hope, sparked by imagination and strengthened by enthusiasm. It is greater than sight, deeper than a dream and broader than an idea. A vision goes beyond the realm of prediction. In fact, it goes beyond anything we can imagine with our finite mind."

It is God, in his infinite wisdom and intelligence, who first places the vision in our hearts. He provides us with just an inkling of his ultimate greatness to be touched gently by an idea that he has. As we take that idea, work with it, and cultivate it, he can begin to shower us with meaningful direction and purpose that is aligned with what he has designed us to do. As we move forward in obedience, he can begin to unveil his plan to us.

As you fully experience the driving force that resides inside the very essence of your being, pushing you and driving you forward, you will become more in tune with what you are designed to accomplish.

At first, the vision that resides in your heart is nothing close to a physical manifestation. An abundance of great work is required for an individual to manifest his destiny. Spiritual insights must be gained through the persistent and sustained concentration of mental acuity. This is precisely why the great Ralph Waldo Emerson once said, "Greater are they who are able to see that spiritual is stronger than any material force. Thoughts rule the world." It is indeed incumbent upon those who desire to achieve greatness to exert their mental powers to the fullest in an effort to materialize the dream.

Consider the fact that the cerebral cortex houses between ten and fourteen billion nerve cells. This is a truly remarkable gift with which God has potentially endowed every human being. How we use those cells is up to us. Indeed, what vast and incredible potential lies dormant there. The more we can utilize our mental powers effectively and fixate on a particular objective over a sustained period of time, the greater the opportunity for that objective to be reached. It then becomes much as William Jennings

Bryan has suggested: "Destiny is not a matter of chance. It is a matter of choice. It is not a thing to be hoped for, it is a thing to be achieved."

If a vision is greater than sight, then heartfelt images transcend the scope of sight. When one echoes Dr. King's sentiments in his incredible "I Have a Dream" speech, one should make every attempt to grasp the full, prophetic meaning of that speech not just for what it meant in 1963, but for its powerful and unequaled relevance to your life now and in the future. When I speak to an audience or when I write, I don't ask people about King's dream, I ask them about theirs. I ask them whether or not they've given any thought to the dreams they have for themselves or for others, and whether or not they have that desire to make a positive difference in someone else's life.

Visions are deeper than dreams. A vision is powerful and personal. It belongs solely to you. It is multifaceted and has many contours, many detours, and numerous uncalculated events that occur between the wish and the fulfillment. Many times they are fraught with tremendous adversity. Do you remember how Joseph's brothers tried to turn his dream into an outright nightmare? And what about Moses's experience when God selected him to remove the Hebrew children from captivity? And what about the desires of Joshua and Caleb when they tried to go into the land of Canaan and take the land that God had promised them? Do you remember how their constituents responded?

I'm very aware of the fact that not everyone has read these stories and knows of their tremendous significance and value. However, the larger issue is that in every phase of life in which you have the opportunity to live your vision, you will have many distractions as life unfolds. There will be numerous naysayers who put up impediments and road blocks to thwart your every move. This is life; what else is new? That is human nature, so stop whining and get on with it.

God doesn't always unleash the total vision he has for an individual's life at the onset; it would be far too overwhelming. He gives it to you incrementally. Can you imagine how Joseph might have reacted, for example, if God had told him, "Well, Joseph, I'm going to make you a king down in the land of Egypt. But first, you will have a dream, and your brothers—yes, your very own flesh and blood—will plot to kill you. In fact, Joseph, they are going to drop you into a pit and leave you there to die. But then, you will be rescued, and you will go to Egypt. And oh, by the way, Potiphar's wife, the current king's wife, will take a fancy to you. When you reject her advances, she's going to take it personally and say you tried to rape her. This will raise the king's ire so severely that you will be thrown in jail."

Do you think for one moment that Joseph would've gotten excited about this supposedly fascinating journey he was to go on? Hardly. In fact, he would probably have said, "I don't think so, God. You can select someone else for this one. I have a lot of other things I need to do."

A vision has to be compelling, and in order for it to be accomplished, an individual must be committed to its fulfillment. In real life, the journey is never easy—in fact, it is a major challenge. It may well take years. The secret to the fulfillment of a vision, if there is a secret at all, is realizing that you have already arrived. It is a mindset. The fulfillment of a vision cannot be vested in the by-products that are received as a result of one's earthly success. These items are only temporal and ephemeral. The real accomplishment resides in the legacy you leave and the value you insensibly set upon your own self-worth. The knowledge you accumulate, coupled with your direct life experiences, plays a significant role in the continuing unfolding of your destiny.

Some people arrive at the threshold of greatness and walk right by, failing to recognize its countenance as well as their arrival because they are either too self-absorbed or fail to appropriately treasure those things in life that count the most.

Although a vision is essential for survival, its seeming unpredictability concerning the events around it causes it to seem incomprehensible at times. It is no wonder that many individuals abdicate their hopes, dreams, visions, and aspirations in despair. Visions are not for the fainthearted. You must possess a tremendous amount of tenacity in order to make that vision a reality. Visions are for those individuals who truly understand the abstract concepts of work, faith, follow-through, commitment, will, and obedience, as well as what it means to activate each of those on a consistent and long-term basis. "Those who would achieve little must sacrifice little and those who would achieve greatly must sacrifice much."

The achievement of a vision not only requires an abundance of knowledge and savvy know how, but it also requires the same steadfast stick-ability that Nehemiah so aptly illustrated when he went about rebuilding the walls of Jericho. He said, "I'm building a wall and cannot come down." No matter what happened, he refused to be distracted from the ultimate purpose for which he was framed. Nehemiah was a man who illustrated in God's eyes that he was full of integrity and trustworthiness, and he withstood his detractors. They meant to do him harm, but he refused to submit to their request. He started the course and finished the task. Because of his obedience, God was able to guide him and provide him with the ability he needed to endure and withstand the cunning savagery of those who sought to thwart his drive to complete his mission.

The great Dwight D. Eisenhower once said, "The supreme quality of leadership is unquestionable integrity. Without it, no real leadership is possible no matter whether it is on a section gang, a football field, in an army or in an office." The ultimate factor in achieving a great vision, then, is to master the quality of integrity and mesh it firmly with the undaunted perseverance of enthusiasm. Why is this so important? It is important because as a great writer once stated, "Enthusiasm goes beyond wealth. It is a zeal for living. It is the force within you that prods you to do your best. It is the expression of dynamic vitality. It is the way you walk, the way you talk. It is the result of your motivation and your physical magnetism and energy. It is that sparkle in your eye, the urgency in your voice, the firmness in your handshake. It is that thing that kindles a fire under your chief aim and turns it into a burning desire."

It was the great Ralph Waldo Emerson who once said, "Nothing great was ever accomplished without enthusiasm."

The difference makers in life all have one thing in common. They have a passion for living, they have a spontaneous zeal for what they do, and when you encounter their presence, you can feel their excitement and the fire of life that burns inside them. Certainly they are willing to share their secrets and ideas for a successful life, if people would only listen and then take the time to apply what they have found to be so knowledgeable.

When Charles Swindoll said, "A vision is essential for survival," his words were in perfect alignment with Proverbs 29:18, which states, "Where there is no vision the people perish." People perish for lack of a Godly word; they perish for lack of aim, for lack of direction, and for a lack of goals. I will conclude this chapter on vision with a powerful quote from the Greek philosopher, Heraclitus. "The soul is dyed the color of its thoughts. Think only on those things that are in line with your principles and can bear the full light of day. The content of your character is your choice. Day by day, what you choose, what you think and what you do is who you become. Your integrity is your destiny. It is the light that guides your way."

The Power of Optimism

Optimism is the faith that leads to achievement. Nothing can be done without hope and optimism.
—Helen Keller

As we progress from infancy to adulthood and beyond, each of us has an opportunity as a result of the beliefs and values we learn from our environment, informed experiences, and book knowledge regarding what kind of an attitude we are going to adopt. Whether or not we care to acknowledge it, we are influenced daily by thoughts, values, ideas, and attitudes of others. As we are influenced, we realize early on that we are in the throes of formulating our own ideas and thought patterns about the choices and ideas that we make and embrace. These habitudes then begin to define who we are.

In essence, we adopt a philosophy of life that rings true to who we are as people. Many of the decisions that we make are contingent upon that philosophy that further informs our experiences. I have always been intrigued by the school of thought that permeates the fabric of our society, and although some of my colleagues have chosen to reside in pessimism, I must admit that I subscribe to the power of optimism.

When the romanticism movement began in Europe with a focus on the renaissance and resurgent focus on music, art, and painting, Margaret Fuller, Henry David Thoreau, Ralph Waldo Emerson, and others ushered in the transcendentalist movement that spread all across America. It was a philosophy that extolled the virtues of rugged individualism, self-reliance, and understanding fully the power of nature and what might be accomplished by a strong work ethic and one's own intuition. Both Emerson and Thoreau were two powerful idealists who were huge proponents behind this movement. Emerson wanted human beings to understand that the more you believed in your own abilities, the more effective and the more successful you could become. Emerson is regarded by many to be one of the most profound and intellectual authors in all of American history. It was Emerson who once said, "for I count him a great man who inhabits a higher sphere of thought into which other men rise with labor and difficulty."

By my own choice, that is where I choose to reside. It is neither right nor wrong; it simply is. Our thinking patterns tend to determine how successful we become in life. Our thinking patterns tend to prompt us in deciding our life choices. Here again, it is Emerson who reminds us that "the ancestor of every action is a thought."

The great watchmaker and auto manufacturer Henry Ford also weighs in on how our thoughts empower us to move forward or keep us stymied at every turn. His astute observation in sharing these insightful words of wisdom is, "Whether you think you can or you can't, either way, you're right." If I know for a fact that I have personally discovered something that works well, I am not at all hesitant to share those ideas with others. What I refuse to do, however, is waste breath with a fool. If someone is trying to make me understand why something doesn't or won't work, when I already know that it does by virtue of my own personal experience, then I owe it to myself to sever the ties with that individual and move on to help those who are truly interested in grasping the truth. I'm not interested in arguing or proving my point when I have already done so by the evidence of my success.

Rest assured that a pessimist will never acknowledge that. A pessimist is too caught up in his own mind of wanting to be right and tear down the dreams of others who've spent the better part of a lifetime building what they have. Optimism is a way of life that can be applied by anyone. Several years ago, when I was working on another book project, I contacted Optimist International and asked if I could include the Optimist's Creed in my book. When they told me that it was in the public domain and that I didn't need their permission to use it, I was ecstatic. Here are the fantastic words of the Optimist's Creed.

The Optimist's Creed

Promise yourself to be so strong that nothing can disturb your peace of mind. To talk health, happiness and prosperity to every person you meet. To make all your friends feel that there is something good in them. To look at the sunny side of everything and make your optimism come true. To think only of the best, work only for the best, and expect only the best. To forget the mistakes of the past and press on to greater achievement in the future. To wear a cheerful countenance at all times and give every living creature you meet a smile. To give so much time to the improvement of yourself that you have no time to criticize others. To be too big for worry, too noble for anger, too strong for fear, and too happy to permit the presence of trouble to invade your beautiful personality.

Several years ago, my sister-in-law, Holly Strom, sent me a fascinating book written by businessman Brian Tracy. It was called *Eat That Frog! 21 Great Ways to Stop Procrastinating and Get More Done in Less Time.* Holly knows the kind of material I enjoy reading, and I appreciate her for that. She is such an amazing and incredible inspiration.

Brian had inculcated into his masterful writing the research findings of Martin Seligman's twenty-two-year study at the University of Pennsylvania, summarized in his book *Learned Optimism*, where he determined that "Optimism is the most important quality you can develop for personal and professional success and happiness. Optimistic people seem to be more effective in almost every area of life" (Tracy, 119).

He further identified four specific behaviors that optimists have.

1. They look for the good in every situation.
2. They seek the valuable lesson in every setback or difficulty.
3. They look for the solution to every problem.
4. They think and talk constantly about their goals.

I won't belabor the point, however you can see how this attitude of positivism plays a significant role in the psychology of human achievement. Pure, unadulterated optimism, coupled with a high degree of confidence due to what you have already proven yourself to be capable of doing, can prove to be a most formidable force. In fact, it could serve as the impetus in getting you to the point where you could foreseeably become virtually unstoppable.

Perhaps you will reach a level of independent thought and action that separates you from the masses of people in life, and you will aspire to reach for the possibility of doing things far beyond the level of mediocrity. It may well become as the great Henry David Thoreau has said:

If you advance confidently in the direction of your dreams and endeavor to live the life which you have imagined, you will meet with a success unexpected in common hours. You will put some things behind, will pass an invisible boundary. New, universal and more liberal laws will establish themselves around and within you or old laws will be interpreted in your favor in a more liberal sense and you will live with the license of a higher order of beings.

Stop Waiting

Stop waiting for things to happen. Go out and make them happen.
—Author Unknown

So, you're the one who's filled with so much passion, vision, purpose, wisdom, scope, and talent in life? You have all of these incredible, amazing, and philosophical ideas that are not only beneficial to yourself but to so many others. And yet day after day, week after week, and month after month, instead of figuring out constructive ways to make others aware of what you have to offer, you become distracted by all the other things you allow to dominate and control your time in life.

Soon, another year passes by, and you've still done absolutely nothing to focus on your absolute goal or purpose in life. Truly it is a sad commentary on the state of things in both your life and mine.

Here's what we have to understand about the events that transpire in our lives on a daily basis. Nothing is going to change until we actually make the decision to do things a bit differently. Until we make the decision that what we have to offer the world is awesome, no one will ever know. Nothing will ever happen; nothing will ever change. We have to become the agents of change. We are the ones who have to take the initiative to make things happen; otherwise, nothing ever will.

That entire responsibility for your project and what you desire to see happen with it lies squarely on your shoulders. Yes, absolutely and unequivocally, the real catalyst for change in your life is you.

Able-bodied and ambition-oriented individuals who have achieved an amazing level of success in life will tell you the hours of practice they have expended, the amount of energy they've invested, and the direction and focus they've had to have. Then you will begin to understand the work ethic that is required to achieve the nebulous thing that is called success.

It has taken me a long time to get to a point in my life where I have finally understood one important factor. It is this: no matter how much I have already accomplished, and no matter how many of my incredible friends and colleagues desire to get together with me and construct plans to move forward to the next level, many people lose the fizzle, that fire of enthusiasm. Life gets in the way, and that's normal; we all have to deal with that. Over the years, we get bogged down, family matters usurp our time, and job-related issues eat up the hours. At the end of the day, all you want to do is rest, relax, and make certain you have enough reserve energy left in your tank to prepare for the next day and stay on your game. Then as you grow older, you watch the days slip by, the limited days you have left in your life. They dwindle ever further, and you can actually feel the sense of urgency creeping upon you because you're constantly aware that not even tomorrow is guaranteed. That's when you realize that you have still not accomplished all that you have set out to do. The bottom line is this: you never will accomplish them until you have decided to make the necessary changes required for you to pursue those dreams and goals you have all but given up on. They are still your responsibility and no one else's.

When all is said and done, it will not behoove me to look back over my life and point my finger at someone else who might have been in a position to help me but didn't. It will do me no good to look at my professional colleagues who meant well but got bogged down in the daily business of life and never called to inspire me, talk to me, encourage me, plan a get together, offer me an opportunity to speak on their program, or sell one of my books. It is no one's fault but my own. If we are to be remembered for our lasting contributions in society, then we are to assume full responsibility for what does or doesn't happen in our lives.

Stop waiting for someone else to come along and be the wind beneath your wings to help you soar to higher heights. Start, continue, and finish the process of getting things done yourself. Start investing your own time, your own effort, your own skills, and your own money. Fully utilize the wonderful technology and those amazing and knowledgeable individuals who are available to you. Develop a specific strategy and a goal-setting plan that will enable you to move far beyond your current circumstances.

Be encouraged by the powerful and impactful words of Dr. Robert Schuller: "If it's to be, it's up to me." That is the bottom line. In order to become successful, you must simply stop waiting. Take action now! Get the word out! Don't stop! Make noise! Build the necessary and essential relationships and connections to promote your product, your service, or your skill. Continue to pursue your very own unique and successful endeavors.

If you have a strong desire to succeed in life, this is the way it must be. There is no other alternative. You have to become the one and only person who ultimately makes life happen. When you have an astronomical dream, you have to be the one who fulfills its purpose and mission, and you must have the tenacity to stay the course until such a time as you have made a success out of all the things that matter and are important to you.

Develop the discipline that is both necessary and essential to keep you moving toward your goal every single day.

Stop waiting for other people to encourage you. Get out there and encourage yourself. Stop waiting for results to come in. Get out there and be the constructive catalyst responsible for generating the results that will make your dream a reality. That is the only way that any individual can achieve eminent and lasting success. The heart of the matter is what envelops the heart that matters. Where is your heart? What does it matter to you? What do you have a strong desire to accomplish?

Where you spend your time, energy, and effort are what matters most to you. Reexamine your own priorities and determine what your next step is going to be and why. How does this fit into your success equation? These are the questions you must ask yourself every day. Make room in your life for the things you have a desire to accomplish. Discipline yourself to say no to those individuals who are constantly pulling you in directions that are counterproductive to the direction in which you desire to go. Resist the temptation to fall victim to the circumstances that are detrimental to your well-being. Remember that if your current environment is not appealing and supportive, it's only temporary. It does not have to be ingrained in your real life or in your subconscious mind, unless you desire for it to be.

Throughout the years, we have seen these phrases countless times: "Success is a journey and not a destination," and "The journey of a thousand miles begins with the first step." They're both true.

The road on which you are now traveling could be the one that will take you toward the achievement of your ultimate purpose in life. It could also be a dead-end. If that's what it turns out to be, you've got to turn around and begin again. Become aware of what's impeding your progress. Have enough respect and value for what you have to give yourself a fresh start.

Having a passion for what it is that you do in life is critical to your mission of achieving success. God constantly places you in a position to understand what it takes to be successful, to learn from your experiences, to refine the process, and to fully understand the skills he has allowed you to acquire in specialized areas. These are more than enough to be the vehicle you are using that enables you to fulfill your ultimate purpose of inspiring others and enabling them to realize their full potential. In other words, what you do every day is not an end in and of itself, but is merely the vehicle you are using that enables you the opportunity to inspire others to move to a higher level of thought and action. What a powerful idea that manifests itself regularly and daily in the lives of others.

It's the thing you already know to be true for your sake and for the sake of numerous others. Each day, you have an opportunity to pour positivity into the lives of poor, despondent souls. You encounter situations where a powerful word of encouragement, an enlightening conversation, a word of hope, or a positive prayer is capable of lifting the spirits of others into a realm they may have not known even existed. This could be the very medicine they need to keep going in life amid the debilitating and desperate crises they face every single day. It was Emily Dickinson who once said, "Hope is the thing with feathers that perches in the soul and sings the tune without the words and never stops at all."

It may be your voice they hear that carries Emily's message straight to their hearts and helps restore some sanity to their already depleted, frustrated, and distressed soul in need of spiritual guidance and encouragement. It is this gift of a kind word that speaks peace and helps them to keep on keeping on in spite of seemingly insurmountable odds. If this is the case, that makes you a difference maker.

Encourage others to understand the fact that life matters and that the very substance of the words you use when you communicate effectively with others are the words that matter most. If you try to drag me down, speak words of bitterness, and sow discontent into the heart of my soul, I will voluntarily remove myself from your presence and replace the void that you leave with the positive reinforcement of another human being. In this way, I can continue moving forward to be a positive difference maker in the lives of others. I refuse to accept anything less than the best, because

Dr. Robert L. Lawson

I have stopped waiting. It was former president of Morehouse College Dr. Benjamin E. Mays who once shared these magnificent words of wisdom.

> It must be borne in mind that the tragedy of life doesn't lie in not reaching your goal. The tragedy lies in having no goal to reach. It is not a calamity to die with dreams unfulfilled, but it is a calamity not to dream. It is not a disaster to be unable to capture your ideal but it is a disaster to have no ideal to capture. It is not a disgrace not to reach the stars, but it is a disgrace to have no stars to reach for. Not failure, but low aim is sin.

The Power of the Mind

Your mind is the gift of creation,
Empowering all that you do.
You can be a true inspiration
If you plan and then follow through.

In your quest to build a great future,
You must challenge yourself every day
By seeking to test your resolve
As you work to secure your way.

The decisions you make will determine
How high you are likely to rise.
Your focus will be a great factor
As you dare to reach for the skies.

For there are no limitations
For a vast and superior will.
The drive and the surge you possess
Create an emotional thrill.

For there lies the true architect
Of the destiny you seek to achieve.
There's so much you can accomplish
As soon as you truly believe.

For this gift with which you are blessed
Is a truly remarkable find.
Nothing can withstand the power
Of a sharp and sagacious mind.

For the mind combined with conviction,

Tenacious persistence, and skill

Defeats it elite competition;

It's the nature of a trained human will.

Purpose

Our thoughts create our reality, where we put our
focus is the direction we tend to go.
—Peter McWilliams

As I endeavor to place on paper those thoughts and ideas that have potential merit to the reader, I always immerse my mind in the work of those individuals for whom I have deep admiration, reverence, and respect. Usually the writers I select are those who make every effort possible to improve the human condition. That is also my own life's purpose.

I remember telling someone a few months back that I thought it was high time I revisited the philosophical statement that serves as a driving force for why I write and speak. It was a statement that I had crafted over thirty years ago. It stated, "My desire is to see, touch, and inspire the hearts of people, making them aware of their worth and value to themselves and to others."

As I examined each word carefully, I recognized that my ultimate purpose in life had not changed. That statement is reflective of the precise core of who I am. That statement is the true north compass of my life. That is what drives me. It's the fire inside of me that keeps me pumped and keeps me moving in what I think is the right direction.

It is my belief that all people need to find their core belief in life and keep at it. I am exceptionally proud of the fact that my purpose statement still serves as the catalyst and the guiding light to which I aspire. Those individuals who have discovered their ultimate purpose or calling have been able to accomplish so much more.

It is incumbent upon all of us to become knowledgeable enough and to understand fully that for many, the unveiling of one's ultimate purpose doesn't always happen overnight. As you mature and as you work in meaningful positions throughout your life, you discover many things about yourself and others that enable you to grow into the person you are to become. The skill set that you master, and each job that you hold, helps you build your character and brings you ever closer to your ultimate purpose.

In the powerful book *The Royal Path of Life*, these words are written. "A man may work in the dark, yet one day light will arise upon his labor; and though he may never with his own lips, declare the victory complete, someday, others will behold in his life's work the traces of a great and thinking mind."

As you contemplate your own life's purpose and the significant impact you may have upon the lives of other people, keep in mind that the tapestry you weave is your contribution to the whole. It blends into the fabric of all of those weavers who have gone before you. Yes, it is time that people heard your story. It is time that people learned vicariously through your successes, along with your failures or errors in judgment. Tell them how you managed to stay the course and pursue your own endeavors in spite of the odds.

People must be made to realize that life is a continuing voyage of self-discovery and understanding. There are many beautiful days, and yet on this life journey, there are also tempestuous and tumultuous storms raging on the sea, seeking to capsize your ship and pull you beneath the sauntering waves. Yet somehow you must learn to adjust the rudders. You must learn to adjust the sails, figure out ways to stand strong in the face of adversity, and remain steadfast, firm, and resolute in your will as you recognize God's original intent for your life through the muck, mire, and missteps.

Each time we develop the ability to learn from the past, we find that it becomes most beneficial in enabling us to create a new and different future, which more often than not places us just a little closer to the goal for which we are striving. When you know that God has endowed you with a rich gift, a talent or skill, or perhaps a vast plethora of them, then you should seek to enhance the quality of your life and hone those skills to the point where thousands or maybe even millions can learn from them and become more adept at what they are doing in life, stimulated to action as a result of how your life and your words intersect with their world and serve as an inspiration and catalyst for their upwardly mobile aspirations.

A noble life purpose can enable an individual to maintain his integrity. When your thoughts, ideas, and actions harmoniously mesh with important matters, your mind seeks to elevate itself to higher order thinking. If those thoughts are repeated often enough, they result in the formation of powerful habits that will propel you in the direction of some of life's finest achievements. A high-level purpose and integrity are brothers who closely resemble each other. They impact each other and are interchangeable. An ultimate purpose can drive a person's integrity just as a person's commitment to a high level of integrity can drive his purpose.

How and what an individual thinks is a constant and determining factor in his level of individual, personal, professional, and societal achievement. Who we are and who we become is solely contingent upon the influences of our mental diets as a result of what we read, coupled with our own life experiences, those individuals with whom we associate, and especially those habits that we develop.

The Greek philosopher Heraclitus once noted, "Abundance of knowledge does not teach men to be wise." This statement suggests that we can have all the knowledge in the world available to us, right at our fingertips. We may even know a lot of it. However, if we do not take the time to put the precepts and ideas into practice, we can still wind up making poor choices. As we do so, we wind up placing self-imposed restrictions upon ourselves, and then we become prisoners of our very own self-indulgence. We allow ourselves to be pulled off course by whims and fancies that take us in a direction of nowhere. Then we begin to flounder and drift as we get further away from our intended purpose. We find ourselves off track. If we are to make any serious life progress, we have to get back on track.

Not only does God supply us with the gift of original thought, but he also provides us with an abundance of information that can enrich and validate our own life purpose from time to time. Here's how it works. Several years ago, I was sitting in a barber shop perusing some old magazines. In the midst of the pile was a wonderful book written by the Reverend Bishop T. D. Jakes. As I picked it up and flipped through the pages, I stumbled across an incredible quote that has since helped to mold and shape my life.

> When you are assured of your purpose, you are not fearful of men nor external personal conflicts that attempt to hinder you, why? Because you know with confidence that sooner or later every trial, every hindering situation, every opposing person and thing in your life will eventually and inevitably bow and submit to God's plan and purpose for your life. It is just a matter of time and circumstance.

What an awesome passage that was for me. Why would I not want to share those incredible words of wisdom and powerful insights with you? The fact is simple: when God has designed you, picked you, and designated you for a specific purpose in life, then no matter what you are experiencing and how bleak your situation looks, simply remember that your current situation is only temporary at best.

With God as your guide, you will ultimately prevail and overcome any adversary who seeks to impede your progress. The fact of the matter is if you desire additional insights regarding purpose or any other topic discussed in this book, God has already prepared for your benefit a myriad of individuals to provide you with the ammunition and empowerment you need in order to achieve an uncompromising level of professionalism, as well as a tremendously fulfilling life.

A part of discovering a person's life purpose requires finding out who one is not. There was a time in my life when I thought I wanted to be a mystery writer like Stephen King or Dean Koontz. Upon reading their books, however, I quickly discovered that I was not the type of writer who had the desire to mystify, horrify, or entertain. That kind of writing is not for me, although I enjoy reading a mystery novel from time to time.

I have concluded that my main purpose in life is to encourage others and help them to understand and realize that they can refine, develop, and enhance their latent potential beyond anything they could ever imagine. Nothing excites me more than knowing that through my books and speaking engagements, people have taken to heart something they've read or heard, and they've put into action some of the concepts and ideas mentioned, as opposed to approaching life in a passive manner and merely existing without having learned to live.

I am not a fiction writer; I am a nonfiction writer. I don't write fantasy novels. I write books that deal specifically with life matters and ways to help people to live life more effectively.

For every individual, life is a little different. No two life paths are exactly the same. Although sometimes there are some similarities, also there are some major differences. One person may know in his heart what he was designed to do from the time he was a child; there are times when this calling is most evident. Others may constantly be discovering who they are daily. In an incredibly amazing book, *Masters of the Situations*, I discovered an intriguing passage from a powerful play written by the great poet Lord Byron.

> From my youth upward, my spirit walked not with the souls of men, nor looked upon the earth with human eyes. The thirst of their ambition was not mine. The aim of their existence was not mine. My strengths, my griefs my passions and my powers made me a stranger.

It has become so obvious to me over the years that each of our places and what each of us has to offer others is incredibly unique. We realize how unique and different we are when we consider all of the raindrops or snowflakes that fall, without two being exactly alike. We understand how different we are when we stop for a moment and realize the tremendous variations that exist among individuals when we contemplate the idea that no two thumbprints are exactly the same.

It is this uniqueness that sets you apart from everything and everyone else. What exactly is your purpose? What are you doing daily to bring it into being? Several years ago, I stumbled across a great quote by Morrine Schwartz.

> So many people walk around with a meaningless life. They seem half asleep, even when they're busy doing things they think are important. This is because they're chasing the wrong things. The way you get meaning into your life is to devote yourself to loving others, devote yourself to your

community around you and devote yourself to creating something that gives you purpose and meaning.

Creating this book for you gives my life purpose and meaning. Who am I? Well, I am a Christian, a teacher, a writer, a father, and a speaker—nothing less and nothing more. These are the things I am. These are the things I do. Many of you are similar in one way or another, and whether or not you plan to, you will leave a legacy. The only question that remains is what your legacy will be.

Focus

*Whatever it is that you most strongly and ardently desire, must
become the centralizing focal point of your thought process.*
—*Dr. Robert L. Lawson*

It is amazing what you can accomplish in life if you develop the ability to focus. There is probably no greater usurper of talents and abilities of people than the lack of discipline to stay with a project until it is finished. Most of us can be influenced easily by others who tend to pull us off task. We are sometimes our own worst enemies.

No one has told us what to do or how to behave, and we therefore find ourselves in conflict with our own priorities. Added to this challenge comes the burden of distractions and unplanned interruptions, but still we must acknowledge to ourselves that we exercise the freedom of choice. That alone is ours. Though it may take a tremendous amount of discipline and courage to use it, we do have it, and quite frankly we can use it to our advantage.

A great writer once said, "Trained thought focused upon a specific goal must not be deterred." The key word here is *trained*. People who train themselves to think properly and adhere to their scheduled regimen of activities and projects on a consistent basis have an amazing advantage over those who are sporadic in their endeavors. If your desire is to become successful, then don't let internal distractions keep coming to the forefront of your mind, and don't allow external factors to throw off your current aim. Of course, you must use rational judgment for each situation, event, or happening, weighing each facet against the others. It is you who should always remain in control of the decisions you decide to make.

If someone wants to focus, a decision will have to be made to establish a certain timeframe for completing a specific project by adhering closely to the rules at hand. This one ability, when practiced with diligence, can increase an individual's output by a thousandfold. Strong discipline of the mind provides the power necessary to rule the other needs of the body and thus the emotion and action process. The mind must govern emotions and actions to yield the results linked directly to a person's progress and status in life. One must develop the ability to discern and dissuade those factors that enter one's thinking process to ask for control of one's time. The more you realize that time is life and that life is limited, the more you will tend to focus on those things that enhance the quality of your life and keep you moving forward.

Possessing a sustained drive to complete a worthwhile project is no easy task. There are, however, a number of reasons that one can use to keep motivated in deciding to complete it.

You should place a special emphasis upon what rewards or opportunities might occur as a result or your sustained effort, not to mention the recognition and the experience you will gain as a result of your endeavor. Focusing already requires a sense of urgency for completion.

A pattern both in thought and action must be formed as a means for actual work to be completed. The responsibility for decision making on any endeavor rests solely with the initiator. It is always an advantage if you have others who can assist you when its gets to a point where you need their expertise. This frees up your precious time to work on these areas where your talent is of the highest benefit and makes the greatest impact.

As in the game of tennis, once you've made the serve, you have completed your portion of the action required. It would behoove your opponent to return the serve, or else you will conclude the match with an early victory in those cases where your skill level is vastly superior to your opponent's. Being able to focus gives direction, credence, credibility, and clarity to the end that you desire to obtain.

When we are able to block out those intrusions that diffuse our thoughts, it creates a much better opportunity for us to focus on our goals. Our increased mobility in the world is determined by how much we are able to accomplish. Our desire to further ourselves and tap into our underutilized and underdeveloped potential can be realized as a result of the time, energy, and effort we invest in improving ourselves.

In order to focus specially upon those things that will propel us forward, we have to be aware of those distractions that serve as a negative influence on what we do. As you reprioritize those things you desire to accomplish, be certain to identify those things that assault your time: television, video games, Facebook, Twitter, texting, sports, and anything else that breaks your power of concentration. This includes the demands that are placed on you by others.

When that happens, you must reexamine your schedule, monitor how you are utilizing your time, and improve those areas that are most beneficial to you so that you have the time for those things you enjoy doing most. When you are considering school, college, a good-paying job, your future, and developing skill sets that will help you to succeed in life, you must force yourself to focus on what all of it means to you. Your status, your position, being able to provide for yourself, your family, realizing your dreams, your goals, your ambitions, and your innate desires factor into your ability and desire to focus.

Being able to focus properly on life assignments is like the well-regulated lenses of a properly adjusted camera. You won't snap the picture until the focus is clear and you have your subject clearly in range. Your ability to focus enables you to direct your energies toward your specific goal. It enables you to utilize and adjust your vision properly until it is directly in your sights.

One of the major keys to developing focus is the development of a specific plan that should be followed precisely and carefully in order that results are forthcoming. The process requires an individual to sit down and reflect on where one is in life and where one desires to go, and to determine the specific route and timeframe that will get the person there (and how reasonable this approach is). Some people have difficulty with this process because it can be frustrating and overwhelming. It may not appear that an end is in view.

Take this approach and break it into fragments. Success in any endeavor is a step-by-step process.

Here's one specific example of how it could work. A young man pursuing his doctorate degree did it this way. There were so many hurdles he had to face when he attempted to complete it. Once he found a program that accepted him, he cleared the first hurdles and began his course of study. His first year in the program, he worked a fulltime job from 8:00 a.m. to 4:30 p.m., and he attended classes away from home on weekends. It was quite a challenge. The next major hurdles were figuring out how to finance his education. Expenses were significant; this was the fall of 1983. He decided to take out a guaranteed student loan and paid the tuition.

During the program, he applied for two additional student loans totaling fifteen thousand dollars. During that time, the maximum amount of money a student could apply for was twenty-five thousand dollars.

The next challenge lay in the fact that this was a nontraditional program, and not a lot of students were involved, so there wasn't a lot of peer support. One had to be very self-motivated to even attempt this program. This meant that a tremendous amount of self-discipline was required. This was especially true when it came to focus on assignments that were due. The rigor of the program, particularly in the area of statistical analysis, didn't make things any easier. There were no ways to gauge how well one was doing until after one had completed a project.

Another challenge included juggling home and work responsibilities, which included spending quality time with a young son, maintaining a good job performance, and placing a low priority on an almost nonexistent social life. If you ever intend to achieve significant worth, sacrifices have to be made.

Another challenge was money spent versus the turnaround time on the review of submitted writings and materials. There was much written correspondence that took place, and great frustration occurred when submitted documents had to be revised or modified before acceptance was granted. The challenge was further compounded by the fact that if your third rewrite on a particular course project was found to be unsatisfactory, you would have to take the entire course all over again. To add additional frustration and trepidation to your field of study, if your professor found your level of work not commensurate with doctoral writing standards, the possibility of your being dismissed from the program was a bleak reality.

Anytime someone strikes out on the road of achievement, all of these are extraneous variables that impact the process. One of the major differences between winners and losers in life is that winners keep on keeping on amid all the distractions in spite of the odds that are stacked against them. It's never the getting off track that stops you. It's the never getting back on. What does the winner do? The winner manages to stay in touch with the struggle, the determination, the tremendous hours of preparation that is required, the dedication, the commitment level, the rehearsal, the long and arduous hours of practice, the belief level, and the practice sessions. Ask any professional athletes what it takes to obtain a level of eminent greatness in this society, and each one will tell you what is required.

Before Michael Jackson became a superstar, I can remember watching him sing on *The Ed Sullivan Show*. At that time Jackson was five or six years of age, but what a talent he had. He continued to cultivate that talent starting at an early age. Even though it is never too late to start, training for excellence should begin at an early age. At the least, the formation of good habits should begin there. The sooner one is able to develop a meaningful sense of direction and purpose, the greater the opportunity for success to occur.

This is not to say that children should not be permitted to be children; it's simply that the formation of good habits at an early age can form the foundation for greater success to occur in later life. It is quite true that some adults today never had a childhood because they had to assume too many adult responsibilities when they were growing up. However, if we allow ourselves to think children should not assume any responsibilities at all, then we are neglecting our own responsibilities by allowing them to be so permissive that they develop a number of bad habits that could be very difficult to break and even become destructive in nature.

The powerful, progressive measures you take for your own future and the lifestyle you desire must be cultivated early on; the future you dream about requires diligent work, a strong work ethic, and certainly laser focus to achieve.

It is much as the co-author of chicken soup for the soul, Jack Canfield, has said:

> Successful people maintain a positive focus in life no matter what is going on around them. They stay focused on their past success rather than their past failures, and on the next action steps they need to take to get them closer to the fulfillment of their goals rather than all the other distractions that life presents them.

Destiny

Taps gently on your shoulder,
Speaks softly in your mind,
whispers in your ear
As you begin your upward climb.
It knows your heart that matters,
For it lives within your soul.
It's woven in your fabric
As you conquer every goal.

As you seek to mold your vision
With a carefully crafted plan,
It calls you to your purpose,
For it knows where you shall stand.
That inner voice that guides you,
Transcends your human will,
Preparing you for mastery
Of things far greater still.

The I AM lives within you,
Empowering you to win,
And nothing can be greater
Than the God that lives within.

Dr. Robert L. Lawson

The Measure of a Man

The measure of a man
Lies in the armor of his will.
It's reflected in his actions
And the power of his skill.

It is his contemplative manner,
And the strength of his resolve,
That will force the proper action
For the problems he must solve.

His intent must be unshakeable,
Immovable in thought.
To bring it to fruition
Will take everything he's got.

True greatness is a quality,
Lying dormant in the soul.
It's the world of negativity
That blocks him from his goal.

To achieve his true ambition,
Though it is a daunting task,
Turn your back upon the world;
You must do nothing that it asks.

Draw from your Godly wisdom
All the things for which you seek.
For the carnal mind of man
Is the thing that makes him weak.

His belief in his ability
will further him the most,
For the gifts that God has given him
Will guide him to his post.

That quality of brilliance,
Residing in his mind,
Is the catalyst for many
And helps to make his life sublime.

For the talent he is holding
In the center of his hand
Is the one that's now unfolding—
It's the measure of the man.

The Run for the Gold

Life is either a daring adventure or nothing.
—Helen Keller

All of us have those memorable moments where we can reach into our treasure chest and pull out a memory when we need that inspirational boost. I'm about to share one with you that would later challenge me to do something interesting that will hopefully benefit someone else. In 1966, I was a sophomore in high school. I enjoyed sports, played football, and ran track. The name of my school was the Southwestern Highlanders. My senior year, I was a starting tailback, and our football team was 7-3 which turned out to be one of the best records in the history of the school. I averaged 9.5 yards a carry, which meant if you wanted to get a first down, you gave me the ball. I also made it to state-level competition in track and field by placing in the long jump. Now, I was no Jesse Owens, but if one could jump over twenty-one feet in high school, that was pretty good, and I could.

The first two Super Bowls were played in 1966 and 1967, and I got to watch both of them on a black-and-white TV because we didn't have color back in those days. Vince Lombardi, coach of the Green Bay Packers, was the colorful master showman during that time period, and the Packers went on to win both of those games. Mr. Lombardi would go on to write a book about that historical experience. It became a best seller, and the title of his masterpiece was *What It Takes to Be Number One*.

Years later, in Columbus, Ohio, I had become a member of the National Speakers' Association and had the opportunity to enjoy a portion of the rich legacy of Mr. Lombardi by hearing his son, Vince Lombardi Jr., speak about his father's vast achievements, his leadership style, and some of his literary work. The most moving part of Vince Lombardi Jr.'s presentation was the memorable moment when he closed his presentation with an incredibly powerful and informative poem entitled "The Race." I remember driving home after that event and thinking, "Wow!" I was truly enamored with that poem as I reflected on the message that it sent, and for some odd reason, I kept saying to myself, "You can do that."

"Do what?" you're probably thinking. Well, I kept thinking that I could write a poem similar to the one I had just heard, and that I could use as an inspirational piece in one of my programs. Years later, I would do exactly that. I didn't call it "The Race," of course, but I did call it "The Run for the Gold." It's amazing, those things that happen to us in life that wind up inspiring us to do things we never thought we could do.

Here it is. I hope you enjoy reading it as much as I did writing it. Indeed, it does have a very powerful message. I won't have to tell you what that message is; it is self-explanatory.

The Run for the Gold

Many and many of years ago,
There's a story that has often been told
Of a boy who desired to please his dad
And decided to run for the gold.

Each time I think of the outcome
On that long ago blistering day,
I find great comfort and solace
When things aren't going my way.

These teenage boys had come from afar,
And the starter had fired his gun.
Each one started out even,
And soon they were off on the run.

The boy who wanted to please his dad
Jumped way out front in the lead.
But a few yards down that rough trodden road,
His foot had started to bleed.

As he sat down to take off his shoe,
He tripped on a rock, and he fell.
The crowd snickered because of his plight,
And he knew he was not doing well.

Though he had fallen back in the pack
And was quite a way from first place,
He spotted his dad who gave a thumbs-up,
And he knew he was still in the race.

So faster and faster and faster he ran;
He tried to catch up with the rest.
He was running almost as fast as he could;
He was giving it all of his best.

He lost his balance, and down he fell;
He landed flat on his hands.
Amid the cheer, you could hear some jeers
Coming straight out of the stands.

But still he got up, and he searched deep inside
To find courage to finish this race.
And just before he gave up in despair,
He spotted his father's face.

"You can still win," his father did shout.
"Just remember the courage to try."
And the boy got up to stay in the race,
Though he felt as if he would die.

He ran and he ran as fast as he could,
So fast that he fell down again.
He felt so despised so dejected, so hurt,
And he knew that he just couldn't win.

But just as a flickering thought of defeat
Filtered across his mind,
He heard his father's voice say,
"Get up, just one more time."

So one more time, up he rose,
And he crossed that line dead last.
And though the crowd cheered hard for the winner,
They cheered harder when the young boy passed.

And when he came face-to-face with his dad,
He hung down his head and cried.
"I didn't do so well," he said.
"I didn't at all, but I tried."

"You are still a winner, my son,
For life is, after all,
Just a chance to redeem yourself,
And to rise each time that you fall."

So let us all take a lesson
From the runner and our friend.
When others try to break your will,
Rise up and try again.

For the goal is not the gold;
Life is more than that, after all.
The simple truth of the matter is just
To rise each time that you fall.

Faith

It's all about believing. You don't know how
it will happen, but know it will.

This moment in time is yours. Step into it and own it like you never have before. Be appreciative and thank God for giving it to you. There is perhaps nothing more powerful than acknowledging the favor which you've been granted and shown by God in his infinite mercy and wisdom. Experience this wow moment in your life like you never have before. Ask God to release his mighty power and magnificence to others through you, and to use you mightily to accomplish his will for your life.

Take time to acknowledge the fact that there is absolutely nothing you cannot achieve or accomplish with God as your ultimate guide and your secret resource and reserve of mighty power. This is something that

I happen to know without one iota of doubt. There is no doubt. I have watched God work his ultimate miracles in my life, and I have observed it firsthand.

When God touches someone's heart to assist you in what he desires for your life, your greatest adversaries have zero power in preventing you from accomplishing your goals. It is literally impossible for you to be stopped. Why? It is simply because your steps have been ordered by God, and the divine destiny that was established and set aside for you is made manifest as God wills it.

God's holy anointing is upon you, and it is his will in the end that always prevails and forces the balance of proper action.

There is always work that has to be done. He makes sure that you have adequately prepared yourself with the right and prerequisite knowledge to fulfill all of your responsibilities and obligations; that too is an integral part of the entire process. The opportunity does not avail itself until you are amply prepared.

In many cases, you may not even know that you are prepared until that exact moment arrives, and yet you will know because God's spirit will reveal it to you at that time. I have been a witness to it again and again in my life, which is why I possess the authority to speak with a conviction that has no comparison.

No one knows you the way God does. This is precisely why I rely totally upon him for meaning, purpose, and guidance in my life. I trust him 100 percent. He is the only one who knows my exact thoughts, actions, and ideas, even before I know each one of them.

I have learned to listen spiritually to his voice, especially in those situations where hard decisions have to be made. Amid all the hustle and bustle of life that can easily cause you to falter, stumble, and get off track, it is at those moments that I ask him to speak directly to my soul and quell my suspicions, my uncertainties. I ask him to provide me with solid decision-making skills that are necessary and essential to keep moving forward. God has never been wrong, not even once.

When you have the opportunity to walk with the Holy Spirit, who finds it impossible to fail, you win.

The essence of the matter is that it's not even about winning. It's simply about you being the best you that you can possibly be when God places you in the opportune position he has given you to shine.

God prepares you daily for his next move for your life. He keeps his anointed hand fully upon you. All ordinary men and women will be able to do is speculate. Had I listened to many of them or taken the time to acknowledge their limited mindset, I would by no means have been able to get where I've gotten today. I refused to acknowledge their limited views for my life, and I made the choice to trust God's guidance and will for my life. It is the greatest decision I've ever made. It gives new meaning to the phrase "You and God are a majority." What's beautiful about that phrase is the simple fact that no one can touch it. It provides you with the illimitable measure of success. You don't have to worry about receiving validation from anyone who does not possess or will ever have the ability to measure up to God's standard for your life. Anyone can place more limitations and restrictions upon you, and sometimes they may even be self-imposed. But at the appointed time, God will remove even those from your life, and they will no longer impede your progress. It is indeed a powerful spiritual thing that is unmatchable. When God is ready to move you forward, simply get out of his way. His might, momentum, and magnificence are not possible to stop. If he wills it, it is done!

What I have made an effort to explain to you, in as clear a fashion as I am able, is God's will for your life. It is faith in action. When you have reached a point in your life where you can trust God 100 percent of the time, you have positioned yourself for great miracles to occur on a regular basis, and the reason why is simple. You will begin to take bold action to assist God in helping you achieve these things you are supposed to be achieving.

When the time is right, God expects you to hold up your end of the bargain. Yes, God expects you to take action, and he expects you to do something. You do not become successful in life by sitting around, twiddling your fingers, and waiting for miracles to happen. Contrary to popular belief, God expects you to make things happen. Mary Cuomo says it this way.

> Faith is risking what is for what is yet to be. It is taking small steps knowing that they lead to bigger ones. Faith is letting go when you want to hold on. It is looking beyond what is for what will be. It is the presence of light in darkness and the presence of God in all.

Remember that God is always there, even when you can't see him, feel him, or know that his presence is close. You can always rest assured that he knows the way. It is his very essence that leads you to the very top of your profession in every single endeavor that he has assigned to you. The magnificent beauty that resides in the whole of it all is simply this: no one can stop it.

The Power of Concentration

Concentration can be cultivated. One can learn to exercise
will power, discipline one's body and train one's mind.
—Anil Ambani

The acquisition of greatness lies solely in the power of concentration. Nowhere has its deliberate obtainment been marked more clearly. For those who succeed in life and for those who don't, the outcome can always be traced back to their private dispositions and the manner in which they pursued their endeavors. The pattern of their success or the lack thereof is told by their ability to master their objectives and own them. For centuries now, the elusive quality for success has been written about and marked indelibly by a man's private manner. All we have to do is follow its clear and delineated path to victory.

Marden has told us, "If we go into a factory where the mariner's compass is made we can see the needles before they are magnetized, they will point in any direction. But when they have been applied to the magnet and received its peculiar power, from that moment they point to the north and are true to the pole ever after. So man never points steadily in any direction until he has been polarized by a great master purpose." Give your life, your energy, and your enthusiasm to the highest work of which you are capable.

As you do this, it will eventually become evident to you that you are in essence preparing and positioning yourself to work diligently in the ultimate purpose for which you were framed. It is this tendency, this bent, or this inclination that will be of the greatest service to humanity.

As you recognize the unfolding of those events taking place in your life to assist you in preparing for the next level of success, you are to achieve the more powerful you will become, and more of your potential will be unleashed for greater service to others.

Your ability to concentrate and focus on those areas that delineate and showcase your most powerful skills will open the magical doorway to assist you in garnering your highest aspirations and manifesting your destiny as it is supposed to be.

Practice your gift, hone your skill, place your creativity into full operation, and use your talent extensively. The day will come when you will be adorned in full array for all the world to see. Your mastery will not be forever hidden because your influence was destined to be greater than you could ever hope to dream or imagine. All you have to do is remain loyal to your conviction and to your purpose. According to Marden,

> The giants of the race have been men and women of concentration who have struck sledgehammer blows in one place until they have accomplished their purpose.

The achievement of great success in the majority of cases has generally been one that requires a tremendous amount of concentration in a given area, coupled with a relentless pursuit of tenacity and spirited conviction. Success at the highest level requires hours of practice in the honing of a particular craft or skill.

We need in-depth knowledge on the specific precision as to how a matter is to be accomplished—and not just through hard work, but work that has been intelligently fashioned and molded so that the results desired will be forthcoming.

It is this mode of operation and commitment that raises the project above its competitors and places it on a level of superior quality that is virtually unmatched. Those individuals who are constantly sharpening their skills, honing their craft, and preparing to advance—while simultaneously drowning out the adversarial distractions, the negativity, and the various annoyances—are those who will emerge at the front of the pack as they climb the steep precipice and complete the race of endurance. As Marden has said, "In all great successes we can trace the power of concentration, riveting every faculty upon one unwavering aim; perseverance is the pursuit of an undertaking in spite of every difficulty; and courage which enables one to bear up under all trials, disappointments and temptations."

It is this triumph of the human will and spirit that destines one for greatness beyond the capacity of limited imaginations.

On Real Leadership

Leadership is the capacity to translate vision into reality.
—Warren Bennis

Those individuals who consider themselves leaders not only know how to accomplish the major milestones that are necessary and essential in their work settings, but they also know how to navigate the stumbling blocks of daily living, which aids them significantly in achieving the results they desire. In fact, it becomes a balancing act where real leaders, over time and through seasoned experience, learn to take those stumbling blocks, turn them into stepping stones, and walk right up the success ladder as prepared as they can possibly be in order to embrace their next high-level assignment.

This does not mean that they have all the skill sets necessary to be fully functional at the next level. It does mean these individuals are poised and ready to assume the next assignment. The key has been their preparation, their willingness to take action, and the confident manner in which they approach their tasks. Their willingness to become part of a new system and their attitude to embrace and learn new ideas that will enable them to grow even more are paramount to their success. That is the art as well as the science of leadership. The art is what you do that makes you an artful master. The science is how you do it. The science of leadership is all about the process. The more you can understand and implement the process, the more effective you will be as a leader.

From a pure and unadulterated perspective, it's all about how you can mesh your incredible and phenomenal skill sets with practical application methodologies that place you in a significant position of strength and enable you to win.

Strong leadership requires strong followship. You cannot be a strong leader until and unless you can get individuals to buy into ideas you are selling. In one of Dr. John Maxwell's books, he makes the following profound and insightful comment. "If someone thinks he's a leader and he turns around to find that no one is following him then he's not really a leader." In fact he's just out for a morning stroll. In essence, he's just taking a walk.

Real leaders remind their constituencies repeatedly about the dynamics of the process on a continual basis. Without those constant reminders, followers have a tendency to revert back to the way they used to do things.

Watch what happens sometimes with major companies when there's a change in leadership, and the new leader brings in his or her new ideas. Sometimes it's effective, and sometimes it's not. Everything is contingent upon how things get done and whether or not the new way of doing things is more effective than the old.

The art of successful leadership is composed of your knowledge base, your mastery of content, and the effective manner in which you deliver it. The science of successful leadership consists of your ability to master the delivery of content through a specialized conceptual framework on process. The science of leadership is all about the systematic approach you use to keep your audience engaged in learning. The more effectively you can manage, measure, and govern this process and mesh together the art and science, the more effective you will be as a leader.

Real leaders learn from their failures and then develop strategies necessary to start over again, with an improved penchant for the things they desire to accomplish most. For them, it's all about the implementation and follow-through process on a consistent basis. The rhetorical question for them becomes, "Can I do what I need to do effectively on a daily basis to close the leaning gap for those individuals who do not yet know what it is I am trying to get them to learn?"

A learning gap is precisely what an individual needs to know in an effort to master a specific idea, but doesn't yet know. The leader who is teaching the concept or idea must vary the teaching approach in those instances where the audience or certain members of it have not yet learned the idea, skill, or information that is being conveyed.

Leaders have educational tool boxes that they must dig into (like plumbers, carpenters, mechanics, architects, and painters have) in order to find the right tool to effectively connect with their audiences. A 9/16-inch wrench will not fit a 1/2-inch bolt. Keep digging until you acquire the right educational tool you need to connect with your audience. Once you make that connection, you will dramatically close the learning gap. The chance for your constituents to gain and apply new knowledge increases. That is your goal. Your educational toolbox contains all of your strategies. It was Douglas B. Reeves who once said, "The word strategy often connotes lofty vision and grand plans in fact, it is simply a method of achieving a result."

Though the abstract qualities of visions and dreams can be powerful and desirable, their value and opportunity to bring them to fruition requires a tremendous amount of effort and systemic creativity. Opportunities themselves are found to be limitless, but it is difficult for average individuals to see them because of their inability to understand the value of the work it takes to make them real. The author Willam James Tilley, who wrote *Masters of the Situation,* said, "Work, work, work is the secret to all great achievement and distinguished success." I would add one sentence to that insightful statement: The work must be intelligent.

Leaders innately know that specific goal-setting strategies, a strong knowledge base, a process-oriented approach, and strong procedures are essential for the achievement of systematic excellence and remarkable accomplishment. Sir Joshua Reynolds once said, "Excellence was never granted to an individual but as the reward of labor. It argues indeed no small strength of mind to persevere in the habits of industry without the pleasure of perceiving, those advantages which like the hands of a clock, whilst they make hourly approaches to their point yet proceed so slowly as to escape observation."

Leaders know that excellence cannot be shaped and obtained without consistent effort, deliberate intent, and an incredible stakeholder accountability factor that lends itself to the integrity of the system and the full consummation of honest means. What you are and what you aspire to be is a continuing work of progress that lends itself to a variety of experiences and life lessons.

Some individuals are astute, observant, and savvy enough to learn from life events. Others are not so fortunate. Perhaps I should say it this way: it's not that they don't learn from them; it's simply that they've allowed themselves to become immersed in bad habits, slothfulness, and indolence. They have developed no desires to pursue anything except unrealistic goals, have developed an aversion for work, and have grown content to do nothing. Unfortunately, it becomes the way of the sluggard. They have learned to merely exist and not live. Their incredible potential therefore lies dormant.

This is precisely why James Allen wrote, "Dreamers are the saviors of the world." In addition, Joseph Campbell said, "A dream is your creative vision for your life in the future. A goal is what you specifically intend to make happen. Dreams and goals should be just out of your present reach but not out of sight. Dreams and goals are coming attractions in your life."

Simply knowing this can provide you with tremendous direction, power, creativity, and precise focus on what you as a leader need to do and should do. Keep moving toward your dreams and goals on a daily basis. Once you are able to get moving in a certain direction, keep moving; that becomes the thing that enables you to get closer to your goal. Every time you plant a seed in the ground for something you desire to see grow, you'll have more opportunities to see a result, especially if you take ample time to water it, fertilize it, tend to it, and cultivate it.

This is an innate characteristic of great leaders. They take the time to surround themselves with other winners. They possess the remarkable gift of recognizing the potential in others, and they want them to develop and grow as well. Real leaders take the time to discuss your strengths with you, and when they observe you in action, they will take the initiative to help you to shore up your weaknesses so that you will become even better at your remarkable craft.

It was Alan Keith who said, "Leadership is ultimately about creating a way for people to contribute to making something extraordinary happen."

Leadership

True leadership requires
A vast amount of skill
As it seeks to service others
And empower the human will.

Leadership inspires,
And it manages to show
A path designed with purpose
and a plan for all to grow.

Leaders make decisions,
And they learn from others too.
They have a focused vision
For the things they plan to do.

They often set examples
For followers to see,
Enhancing ways to cultivate
And serve with dignity

Leadership is work
And a highly poised art
Designed to change your thinking
And captivate your heart.

Its soul contains integrity,
Tenacity, and scope,
With efforts to inspire the world
With confidence and hope.

Through passion and persistence,
A leader's major role
Seeks to serve with honor
And to guide you toward your goal.

With fierce determination
Through turbulence and calm,
In the quest to build potential,
A leader marches on.

So give deep thought to thinking
As you set out on your quest.
You ought to be encouraged
To do your very best.

True leadership is character
Personified each day,
Reflected in decisions,
That you make along the way.

Each outward action taken
Reveals the silent you
And demonstrates your character
In everything you do.

Your mind and high endeavors
Will be tested every week
To expose your true commitment
To acquire the things you seek.

How you relate to others

As you utilize your skill
Will be a major factor
As you exercise your will.

How strong is your resolve?
Can you run this awesome race?
Or will you meet your fate
As you fall upon your face?

And if your face gets bloodied
As you journey down life's track,
Will you lift your head with courage
And still keep fighting back?

For the only thing that matters
To a wise old gal or lad
Is knowing in your heart
You gave it everything you had.

No Limit Thinking

I've learned that fear limits you and your vision. It serves as blinders to what may be just a few steps down the road for you. The journey is valuable but believing in your talents, your abilities, and your self-worth can empower you to walk down an even brighter path. Transforming fear into freedom – how great is that?
—Soledad O'Brien

Take the lessons you can learn from your negative experiences, and allow the positive ones to guide, shape, and develop your character into the person you must become as the prerequisite to the fulfillment of your destiny. Develop the mind you need to succeed through the power of autosuggestion, where you take the time to originate and focus specifically upon thoughts and ideas that will forcefully propel you toward your goals.

This tremendous power that you have at your fingertips can transform every aspect of your life. By repeating and then acting on those powerful ideas, you can sublimate your specific aims toward inexorable ends. This ability that you possess to master the direction of your mind is perhaps one of the most powerful tools you have at your disposal, and the more consistently you are able to act upon it, the more effective you will become at obtaining the results you desire most.

The only limits you have on what you might be capable of accomplishing are generally self-imposed. Most individuals take virtually no note of the fact that their thinking is limited, and so it is no wonder that many cannot achieve their goals. They simply do not know that in order to do so, they must first change their negative thought pattern, which only produces negative behaviors and outcomes.

Stop self-sabotaging your own success. This unfortunate predicament in which the majority of individuals find themselves comes as a result of the predispositions of the very environments in which they are raised. Individuals are greatly affected by their environments and the influences in those environments. It begins when they are still in the womb.

When you arrive in the world, you are immediately exposed to those values and societal factors, and you develop either a scarcity mentality or an abundance mentality. Whichever you choose determines your reality in life. However, it doesn't have to remain that way; you have the power to change what is happening in your life simply by changing the way you think, your disposition, and your attitude about what you want your life to look like and what you are willing to do about it.

Our environments expose our limitations and seek to imprison us within our own minds. Breaking free of limited thinking is the first key toward the obtainment of unlimited success.

You begin to think and act a certain way and if your perception of yourself is that you are limited in certain areas, that begins to shape who you are destined to become.

The beliefs and values you have internalized make up that whole fabric of your character and form the very foundation of who and what you will become in life as you progress through it daily.

What individuals must learn and acknowledge is that no matter how limited their thinking is in terms of what their lives are and how things could be at any given point in time, all of that can change.

It is always possible for an individual to have a significant emotional experience, encounter another individual who is able to make you think in a way you've never thought before, or read a book that expresses things to you in a way that causes you to be motivated to try things you've never done before. Many life-changing experiences have occurred in that manner.

This new experience, whatever it is, can create an internal paradigm shift, a new way of looking at things. It increases your belief level in yourself and what you are capable of doing. This change in thinking is what enables you to step outside the self-imposed box in which you have been living.

Your new perception of yourself and of the world is this first glimpse of an individual who has revealed a new level of thinking in life that is virtually unlimited. It is at this juncture that the world becomes your oyster. No longer do you feel trapped by thinking that you can only make a certain amount of money or be relegated to living in a certain area. Suddenly, you realize that by mastering your own discipline and creative abilities, and by beginning to develop a strong work ethic and utilize your God-given talents, skills, and abilities to the utmost, virtually anything you desire in life is possible.

The funny thing is that some people are able to accomplish more in life than they ever thought they could—simply because someone else believed in them more than they believed in themselves.

The bottom line is this: in order to achieve high levels of success in life, you must firmly and solidly develop the habit of no limit thinking.

It is also critical that you focus less on competing with others and more on competing with yourself, improving a little bit one day at a time. Why? Because you are the answer to your own problem; the real game lies within you. In order to succeed masterfully in life, you have to start competing with yourself. This is where real winning comes to fruition. The only real accomplishment in life comes when you get to the point where you can become the very best you can possibly be. Keep pushing yourself on a continual basis.

It sounds ridiculous to say this, but I must. No matter how hard you try to become someone else, you can't. When God molded you, framed you, and made you, he put the original stamp of endorsement upon the only you in the universe. You simply have to be you.

God made and designed each and every single one of us for a specific plan or purpose. Many times we choose to follow our own plans through free will. Even though we sometimes veer off course and get off track, it doesn't mean that we can't get back on track.

The sooner you realize this and the more clearly your experiences reveal this to you, the more effective you will become in your life as you set out to do exactly what you were destined to do. Become a no-limit thinker and embrace the idea that absolutely nothing is impossible. This new attitude and way of looking at things can catapult you into an arena where you realize for the first time that your imagination truly is the greatest nation on earth. You have no limits.

Just Be Yourself

So many people struggle through life;
They try to be something they're not.
Just make an effort to be yourself.
At least, that is what I was taught.

The more you try to be someone else,
The more confused you will be.
At times you will find yourself asking yourself,
"My gosh, is this really me?"

Sometimes we try to please our friends,
Our family members, and all.
The more we try to keep up the pretense,
The harder and faster we fall.

We try so hard to put on a front,
And the mask we wear hides our eyes.
The fear and failure thoughts in our mind
Remain hidden beneath all the lies.

Then one day the truth comes marching out,
And your soul is finally free.
Then you can say to the ones you love,
"This is the genuine me."

If I've learned one lesson in life,
It's to place that mask on the shelf.
Instead of trying to be someone else,
I'll try harder to just be myself.

The Power of Consistency

It's not what we do once in a while that shapes
our lives. It's what we do consistently.
—Tony Robbins

Anthony "Tony" Robbins mentions a powerful fact in his book *Unlimited Power*: success leaves clues. When you take the time to delve into success literature that has been written, and you examine the lives of those individuals who have managed to achieve high levels of success, you will uncover a plethora of attributes possessed by the majority of them.

For years, until multiple back surgeries, knee surgeries, and a public persona that took a severe beating from an image perspective, Tiger Woods was the most dominant player on the golf course. Not since the days of

Jack Nicklaus had anyone seen anything remotely close to his level of dominance in the game.

When looking at the rationale for that kind of continued success over a period of years, one must take into consideration certain facts with a certain one being that the peak of his incredible and amazing career, Tiger Woods was one of the most consistent golfers to ever hold a club.

To observe and understand Woods' phenomenal rise to the top of the profession, one has to look beyond the number of tournament wins and observe where he finished during those times he didn't win. Therein lies one of the most strategic revelations to the success of Tiger Woods. Those of us who will take the time to apply the idea of being consistent to our own lives will begin to note a vast improvement in those areas where consistency is treated with the dignity and the respect that it deserves. Anthony Robbins validates its primary importance for all of us when he says, "Anything you consistently improve, you will wind up dominating."

How would your life change if you made the decision to embrace this principle? What would happen if, instead of giving up in despair, you made a conscious decision to press on through the slumps, the down times, and the negative comments that everyone else says about you, and you remained consistent to improve on all or many of the endeavors in which you are involved? What would be the final outcome?

What do some of our greatest philosophers and thinkers have to say about this? What do our modern-day writers and authors have to say? Actually, they have much to share with you as they illuminate these ideas for you to consider. Let's take a serious look at how the power of consistency could play out remarkably in your life.

As you read on, look for the powerful role that consistency could play in both words and deeds.

Shortly after my grandmother's death in 1982, I happened to be walking through the house in which we lived when I was a child. Most relatives had gone through and taken things of notable value, but unbeknownst to them, they had left the greatest treasure for me. My foot accidentally kicked an old book that was lying in the middle of the floor. Curious, I reached down and picked it up. And as I leafed through the pages, I noticed several things. First of all, the copyright date on the book was 1889. The title was *Masters of the Situation: Some Secrets of Success and Power.* The book contained chapters on enthusiasm, purpose, manners, habits, city boys, country boy, application, genius, ideals, and numerous other topics.

I think the thing that caught my eye the most was a chapter on possibilities. I turned to that chapter, and as I began to read, my eyes fell upon these words: "It is probable that not one individual out of a thousand has an adequate conception for what he is capable of doing. The possibilities that lie before anyone would probably astound them if they knew at any one moment what they were. Your future is ever before you. Possibilities ever await."

Dear reader, do you find these words written in 1889 both astounding and inspiring to your own heart and soul as you read them now? Do you believe that it is possible for you to do more with the life you are currently living? Then keep reading, and let's see if we can further validate the timeless truth of the power of consistency. Creating new and innovative ways of doing things and adding to your storehouse of knowledge base can provide you with new skill sets and aid you by helping you to significantly improve your financial base. Obviously, this is a desired result that will give you the latitude and flexibility you need to do additional, incredible, and powerful things.

I continue to search for amazing and well-established life connections so that I can help paint a picture that people can see and learn from. Here's how it works.

In 2005, Dr. Stephen Covey wrote another masterpiece entitled *The Eighth Habit: From Effectiveness to Greatness.* The book's primary focus lies on finding your voice, discovering your purpose, and developing your talents and skills in order to fully become the person you were designed to be. How do you do this? You do this through the development of the qualities of integrity, trust, and most important through the discipline of execution. You don't simply talk about making things happen—you ensure that they do. This is one of the major keys to any success event in life. Your ability to deliver is one of life's most effective success tools.

I have read the book, and it is powerful. I am making a conscientous effort to take many of the ideas I have learned and put them into practice. There was one particular quote that has significant relevance to what we are discussing in this chapter. Dr. Covey had unearthed a wonderful quote by Gandhi: "The difference between what we are doing and what we are capable of doing would solve most of the world's problems." What I'm curious about is whether you are able to connect the dots and see the significance between the quote stated in 1889 and the one verbalized in 2005. If not, keep reading. Maybe you'll get goosebumps like me.

Jack Canfield and Mark Victor Hansen co-authored the phenomenal best seller *Chicken Soup for the Soul,* which has since spun off numerous other books. Not only have I had the distinct pleasure of personally meeting Dr. Covey, but I also met both of these distinguished authors and speakers at a seminar they were conducting in Minnesota as part of the 1995 National Speakers Association's National Convention.

Mr. Jack Canfield has since authored other books on his own, but one that he put on the market in 2005 is entitled *The Success Principles: How to Get from Where You Are to Where You Want to Be.* He offers some exceptionally sound advice to others through meaningful stories, analogies, quotes, and experiences. For all intents and purposes, especially for this writing, Jack shares a quote he discovered from one of the world's most famous and ingeneous inventors, Thomas Alva Edison, at the beginning of the book. "If we did all the things we are capable of doing, we would literarily astound ourselves."

Hopefully now you can see the impact that consistency has upon one's talent, skill, ability, or thought process. Perhaps you might even ask yourself the same questions from which numerous others have drawn key insights, inspiration, and wisdom. What am I capable of doing? What would be the result If I continue to polish, hone, and utilize my skills?

As we continue to study these individuals who've achieved high levels of excellence in our society, perhaps we will be able to see how consistency plays a major role by permeating every fabric of their lives and making each one of them just a little bit better at what they do. It's indeed my fervent hope and belief that the powerful concept of consistency can also be extended and utilized extensively and effectively in all of our lives. There is still so much for each one of us to accomplish.

Reflective Thinking

Reflective thinking turns experience into insight.
—John C. Maxwell

I have gone to the woods to do some much-needed reflective thinking. It seems the older I get, the more I develop an affinity for communing with nature. I have grown so much more appreciative of God's wondrous and magnificent creations. The actual quietude of the moment seems to heal the mind and bring more clarity, purpose, and focus to the forefront of your mind. The power you have all around you becomes more evident, and the even greater power that is inherent within you can be felt. You have the power to control your own destiny. It is you who must make an activated decision to do just that. It is comforting to your mind to step away from the cares and obligations that consume you, even if just for a moment. It is this moment of reflection that can help you to regain your much-needed sense of balance and enable you to cope more effectively with those issues confronting you.

It is at this moment that I am observing the motion of the waves as the sun shimmers down upon them. I am watching a family work in unison as they paddle a canoe. I am hearing the busy trucks on the nearby highway, an occasional croak from the frogs, and the chirping of the birds. As a kid growing up, I used to be fascinated with the study of ornithology. I could tell you at one point every type of bird that made its way into our yard, whether it was a blue jay, a robin, a wren, a sparrow, a canary, a red-winged blackbird, or a quail. What's cool is that when you focus, you can recognize and distinguish the various sounds made by each type. When you think about it, that's how it can be with anything you have a desire for in life.

I can smell the fragrance of the surrounding trees and feel the soft, stirring breeze as my senses are heightened. I am watching a beautiful, yellow monarch butterfly fluttering across the winding creek. I'm feeling the coolness of the shade and the comfort of the table on which my arms are placed as it provides the support I need to write freely and describe this personal experience. I see and feel this as one of the many blessings that I've grown to appreciate as a part of life's longevity. I am indeed an incredibly fortunate man surrounded by the God consciousness that exists around me and, even more important, within me.

I am at ease. My mind is full of peace and serenity, and I feel as though I can write with the flow of freedom. At this very moment in time, I am writing how I feel right now, which is very good. Life is filled with ups and downs, but every once in a while, one is able to pause and enjoy a valuable moment.

I see an attractive lady walking. I hear her sandals slapping against the road. Her reflection appears in the water beneath the bridge as she crosses it. The sky is blue, the sun is shining, and there are a few white clouds traveling by at their own pace. I am reminded of God's goodness.

I have been invited to God's own paradise, and the best part of it is that the price of admission is free. The awesome feeling that I have for God's grace and the magnanimous beauty of nature is something that I cannot find the appropriate words to express. I am honored and humbled by his presence, and I can feel it in his creations. I am thrilled to be an observer in God's world, to experience for just a moment the ultimate purity in this way of thinking, and to know that with God's wisdom as my guide, there are no limitations.

Three children have come to play on the nearby bridge. One girl is dressed in blue jeans with a yellow top. Another girl is wearing tan pants and a blue top. A little boy has on a blue shorts outfit. They lean over the bridge, watching the water flow beneath it; they talk quietly and move across the bridge and up a hill. The little boy is carrying a skateboard. They are still talking quietly but have now moved out of earshot. I watch God's creative display unfold before me, and I am enamored by all of it.

The more in tune I become with nature, the more I watch and listen for God's clues as he continually unveils his purposes and magnificence for a fulfilling life. Again, what an awesome thing. A song from a childhood remembrance floods my mind: George Beverly Shay's tribute to God, "How Great Thou Art."

Things are beginning to get good as God unfolds even more of his natural pictures, beauty, and grace before my very eyes. Two ducks, one with a bluish head and gray body and one with tan feathers, have just emerged from the water and approached the table where I am sitting. Right now I am watching in a fascinating trance. It is a beautiful sight. They are not running away but are merely looking and preening their feathers.

A cute couple has entered the picture with their fishing poles and music, situated on a picnic table nearby. They have cast their poles in the water, no doubt waiting for a nibble. The traffic continues to flow on the nearby road, and the ducks have moved on. I'm still in a state of ecstasy, wondering what will happen next.

Amid the hustle and bustle of daily living, try to remember the importance of getting away from it all from time to time, just to hear yourself think. The quietude and graceful state of the mind provides a much-needed balance to life. From time to time, we all need that peace, serenity, and calmness. These are not just words; they are states of mind that lead to states of existence. They are qualities that replenish and refuel us as we strive to climb that next mountain that lies just over the horizon, waiting to challenge us.

These trips we take into paradise provide an opportunity for us to think, examine a particular issue from a distance as we snap back to reality, and reflect on it. Perhaps our creative juices can kick into gear, and we can come up with a fresh approach to an old problem. Perhaps we can come up with a new paradigm or a different perspective on things. The strength we can gain from these scintillating experiences is just like the goal achievement opportunities available to us daily: they are limitless.

Breaking Through

Hard work is about training yourself to leap over this barrier,
tunnel under that barrier, drive through the other barrier,
and after you've done that, to do it again the next day.
—*Seth Godin*

Achieving high levels of success requires an unprecedented belief in the self that enables you to break through all barriers of limitation and resistance. In order to be amazingly successful, you simply have to find a way to do that.

In all instances, it requires a plan of action that you follow through and up on. It can't just be about wishful thinking. It requires you to take the initiative to do things that you perhaps have never done before. You must be willing to take some risks, and you may need to ask people to work with you that you've never worked with before.

Stepping out and being bold often requires doing things differently. You can't expect to do the same things over and over and get a different result. The new thing that you try might be the one thing that sets you apart from all others. After all, it was Helen Keller who said, "Life is a daring adventure or nothing." Sometimes in order to make a huge difference or to establish that connection that you've never had before, you must step out of your comfort zone. This is how you go about breaking through.

You may need to find people who have the skill sets capable of helping you advance your career or business endeavor in a way you've never thought of before. You may need to actively approach others to close a sale.

There are indeed so many things we have to think about and reflect on daily. Like me, when you get stuck in a particular mode of thought or your enthusiasm wanes, ask yourself some revealing and soul-searching questions.

What is stopping me?

Why am I not successful yet?

What haven't I tried yet that perhaps I should?

Is this what I really want to do?

That last question is tricky. In order to break through, you may need to keep doing what you are currently doing because that may very well be your only source of income. Guess what? You need that. Don't give that up until your footing is solid enough to move forward on your new dream or aspiration. There's an old adage that is sound advice for all of us: "Work from where you are with what you have until you get to where you want to be." I'm not about to give up something solid, steady, and income producing for empty wishes and dreams of derelict. Work is what provides incredible substance, puts food on the table, and pays the bills while we build in other areas. Smart people keep a steady head and remain focused as they move ahead in other areas.

Decision making is a key component in whether an individual achieves success or failure. It was Henry Ford who once said, "Failure is nothing more than an opportunity to begin again more intelligently." Those are some of the truest and most powerful words ever written. All that most of us want to do anyway is leave some good advice for those who choose to follow after us. That's what this is all about.

In other words, you become successful because you decide to become successful. It was the empowerment speaker and motivational guru Anthony Robbins who once said, "It is in your moments of decision that your destiny is shaped."

There are so many powerful qualities that an individual must have in order to break through. Decision making is one of them. Another is persistence or determination. How badly a person decides to accomplish a particular thing plays a very significant role in determining whether or not it gets done. Former President Calvin Coolidge was adamant about this.

> Nothing in the world can take the place of persistence. Talent will not. Nothing is more common than unsuccessful men with talent. Genius will not, unrewarded genius is almost a proverb. Education will not; the world is full of educated derelicts. Persistence and determination alone are omnipotent. The slogan 'press on' has solved and always will solve the problems of the human race.

The more competent you are, the more confident and more successful you will become. One begets the other. It is a process that works as you continue to work the process continuously and consistently.

There is a tremendous amount of power that lies in the concept of differentiated thinking. When you've tried doing things one way and it doesn't work, eventually you will have to change your approach and your entire way of thinking and doing, implementing changes that can possibly move you closer to your goals and dreams.

New actions produce new results. Understanding this is critical to getting you close to where you need to go. Success occurs as a result of an accumulation of concerted efforts and actions. It consists of a lifelong process of learning, doing, and unlearning bad habits that hold you captive. Let bad habits go and form new ones that get you unstuck and keeps you moving in the direction you need to go. That is what success is all about.

Alexander Graham Bell said, "What this power is, I cannot say. All that I know is that it exists and becomes available only to a man or a woman who is in that state of mind where he or she knows exactly what he or she wants and is fully determined not to quit until they find it."

There is a powerful poem that I ran across and put to memory years ago. It will lift your spirits during the toughest times.

Don't Quit

When things go wrong as they sometimes will,
When the road you're trudging seems all uphill;
When the funds are low and the debts are high,
And you want to smile but you have to sigh.

Don't give up though the pace seems slow,
You might succeed with another blow;
So stick to the fight when you're hardest hit.
It's when things seem worst that you mustn't quit.

—Anonymous

This is exactly the success prescription you need that will get you where you desire to go. Every single day of your life that goes by, you have to focus exactly on what it is that has helped you to win. When all is said and done, what you have done is greater than what you or anyone else has said.

It will be stated by what you have achieved,

The lives you have touched;

What you have believed,

And your legacy and such.

You decide what success is for yourself because the true definition of success is different for every human being on the planet. Don't measure your level of success against how much better you are than someone else. Instead, measure success against yourself in terms of how much progress you've made today in comparison to yesterday. If there are some setbacks and you had to take a step or two backward before you could start moving forward again, don't let that be the end of the world. That's not what stops most people. What stops most people is never getting back on track. Remember, other people can only stop you temporarily. You are the only one who can do it permanently.

There is only one way that you will ever come remotely close to manifesting your destiny: completing your purpose and doing exactly what it is that God intended you to do in the first place. That means never stopping believing. In other words, you follow the desire that lies within your heart, the one that you feel is constantly tapping at your shoulder, saying, "This is what you should be doing." Live that dash called life like you've never lived it before. Understand and know that it is the relentless pursuit of your goals and dreams that will get you there.

Drive

The road to success is not easy to navigate, but with hard work
and passion, it's possible to achieve the American dream.
—*Tommy Hilfiger*

Whether it's a physical manifestation of one's ability to exert force and energy from an external perspective or a deep-seated psychological belief that originates from an internal feeling, drive can serve as a powerful tool in life for getting things done.

When it comes to accomplishment, whatever it is that you truly desire, or whatever it is that you want to see manifested in life, must become the centralizing focal point of your thought process. Let's take it one step further: you must be driven.

Your ability to network with and convince others by showing them what the fruits of their labor can result in also plays a significant role in your ability to be massively successful to the point where you are able to reach millions of people with your skill sets, your ability, your products, and your powerful ideas as you move forward. That idea or thought can usually be the catalyst that provides you with the impetus, the energy, and the drive to continue moving forward.

The internal passion, coupled with your knowledge base and skill to make a difference in the lives of others, has immeasurable value and may suffice to keep you motivated to accomplish your objectives and your purpose as you develop and expand the connections you have that will inevitably bring your dreams to fruition on a local, national, or international level. Never place limitations upon yourself; you may well be able to go a lot further than you ever thought you could. You have in your power at this very moment a once-in-a-lifetime opportunity to make it happen, and it is essentially your responsibility to do it.

The platforms that are necessary and essential to propel you into the limelight are available and waiting for you. Your job is to capitalize on the resources available to you by reflecting on those connections you already have that are in place to support you and make every effort you can to significantly expand your base by effectively using your current resources.

Every day that you have the ability to get up and move forward, you are living those moments that were given to you by God. These are your moments as of this very instance. Take advantage of these moments and be of service to as many as humanly possible. Right now, you have that once in a million opportunity to grab life by the throat and run with it. It is essentially your responsibility to do so, no one else's.

If your desire is to be incredibly effective in the lives of others, then you must show them decisively that the only reason for their lack of success resides inside of them. When you can get them to realize that they already possess the power and ability to change their current circumstances, then you have something that people want. More important, you have something that they need, and they will buy it. If there ever was a secret to success, that is it. People need what you have to offer, which will enable them to better their lives and get them into a position where the decision making they do will be the thing that improves the quality of their lives. It must be fueled by desire. The power of desire that lies hidden deep within the human heart will continue to help resolve many of the problems inherent in our society today.

Right now, I'm thinking of one of the best ways to illustrate this important point. How bad you want something is the determining factor in whether or not you will ever achieve it. Has anyone ever tried to hold your head underwater for any length of time? What happened? What did you do? Isn't it amazing what you will do to get your next breath of air? The more desperate you become to do so, the more you will start kicking, flailing, biting, and pinching to throw off the individual holding you down. All of a sudden, you get that adrenalin rush, and you start fighting fiercely against the force that's making an effort to stop you from breathing. At that moment, you realize how precious life is, and you want to take that next breath because you're running out of air.

I almost drowned once when I was nine years old. I was in a lake and didn't yet know how to swim. How did that happen? As a kid, my neighbors had one of those inflatable pads that one could push into the water and lie on. Obviously, I wasn't thinking about the consequences, and so I got on where the water was shallow and proceeded to float.

Lying on my back with the sun beaming down felt fantastic. I was caught up in my own little world. Before I knew it, I had drifted into the middle of the lake, where the water was slightly over my head. Then the worst possible thing that could have happened, did! I moved a certain way while I was on top of the float, and the darn thing capsized.

Suddenly, my mouth was full of water, and I couldn't even scream for help. I heard later that a couple of my friends were watching and started toward me. Had it not been for God's intervention, I'm not sure I would have made it. It wasn't my time to go yet. Miraculously, somehow my feet found the bottom of the lake, and I came walking out of the water toward the beach. Needless to say, I've never placed myself in that position to ever have that experience again. That was a very scary moment in my life. I was only nine and didn't want to die. I thank God for saving my life.

I've read both of Les Brown's famous books, and he's a very powerful motivational speaker. One of his books is entitled *Live Your Dreams*, which is exactly what all of us should be doing. The other is entitled *It's Not Over Until You Win!* That is the attitude each of us should have, and it's certainly the standard to which all of us should aspire. Sometimes you have to stand up inside of yourself and silence those voices that keep trying to tell you what you are incapable of doing. It is exactly like Les Brown has said: "you must simply start saying yes to your dreams, yes to your life and yes to your future." Over the years, Les Brown has inspired me tremendously. I've had the pleasure of meeting him and talking with him. He's a good man, and his life purpose is quite similar to mine.

Dr. Wayne Dyer, another one of my top authors, said, "Inspiration is your ultimate calling." He even has a book published by that title. I too desire to inspire others, and like my friends Harvey Alston, Mark Anthony Garrett, Ella Coleman, Gene Murphy, Chad Mckibben, Dr. Jeffrey Fisher, Mike Jennings, Aleta Mays Polley, Holli Pellman, Darian Pellman, Barbara Reynolds, and Margaret Bernstein, I desire to help people to be the best they can possibly be. I don't want to see them move into "settle for estates" when they can be and do much, much more with their lives.

Perhaps the questions that you should be asking people are these. How much time, how much energy, and how much effort are you willing to exert or spend to improve your lot in life so that it becomes a lot more? How strong is your desire? How deep is your drive and determination? How badly do you really want a certain thing?

Les Brown is quite right. The first time I heard that man speak, after he finished, I felt like I could run through a brick wall. I felt like nothing could stop me. He had spoken for about an hour, and yet it seemed like only seconds. I was deeply involved in what he was saying. I wasn't just hearing—I was actively listening.

Then he began to close down his program. It was a standard close that I've heard many times since, but on this particular occasion, it was the first time I had heard any of those words. Here's the thing: you simply do not know when someone is going to say or do a particular thing that, from that moment forward, deeply impacts your life in a profound way. That was one of those moments in my life. When will something like that be a moment in your life?

Perhaps you are wondering what words I am referring to. I won't keep you in suspense any longer. As Les Brown closed his program, he left each of us with these wise, scintillating, and profound words of wisdom from Berton Brailey. Perhaps you may find them as inspiring, powerful, and moving as I did. Perhaps they can turn out to be the difference maker for you. Again, the question is all about how deep is your drive or your love for something or someone. How bad do you want it?

These are Berton Braley's famous words.

> If you want a thing bad enough, you've got to go out and fight for it, work day and night for it, give up your time and your peace and your sleep for it. If all that you dream and scheme is about it, if life seems useless and worthless without it. If you'll gladly fret for it, sweat for it and plan for it, lose all your terror of the opposition for it. If you'll simply go after that thing that you want, with all of your capacity, strength and sagacity, faith, hope and confidence and stern pertinacity. If neither cold, poverty, famine, nor gout, sickness nor pain of body and brain can keep you away from the thing that you want, if dogged and grim you beseech and beset it with the help of God, you will get it.

The Rhythm of Life

Let your life be guided by greatness.
—Matthew Kelly

At age sixty-seven, I still find this life journey fully fascinating and illuminating each step along the way. I'm still enamored by it and am filled with an incredible abundance of enthusiasm and exuberance in this moment as I write. Isn't this in all a part of the secret of living a successful life? Isn't it a powerful thing to be filled with a deep appreciation and a thankful spirit for all that God has provided for our enjoyment and for this evaporating moment in time? I am most grateful for not only the things I've acquired but also for my attitude of abundance toward life.

My commute to and from work is over an hour each way. That's how it has been for the past twelve years. This morning as I rose at 4:30 a.m.

and began my drive at 5:00, for some odd reason I became acutely aware of everything in the center of my universe. When I put the key in the ignition, turned it, placed the car in motion, and turned on the top hits of "Rock a Bye" and "It Ain't Me," I became engulfed in the lyrics. As my car started rolling, I could feel the comforting, soothing, rolling rhythm of life.

Sometimes when I get into that zone where it feels as though I'm floating on the road, instead of allowing the music to progress to another less enjoyable song, I will turn the knob back to replay certain songs that enable me to maintain the mood and flavor of the moment. I love being in that moment.

It is that mystical, magical moment that engulfs the eternal, blissful fabric of your being. As you drive, listen and reflect on the most engaging, climactic moments of your life, such as being one with your significant other, those special times become euphoric, sensual, and deeply meaningful and spiritual. Your past intertwines with your present, and your future greets you as you pass through the present to meet it and accept its warm embrace.

It was Mihaly Csikszentmihalyi, in his masterful book *Flow*, who said, "Mystical heights are not obtained by some super human quantum jump but simply by the gradual focusing on the opportunity for action in one's environment which over a period of time results in such a perfection of skills and becomes so thoroughly automatic that it seems spontaneous and other worldly."

It is at that moment—when your creativity reaches its peak, your awareness of your surroundings and every event that occurs is keen, and your level of awareness is so razor sharp—that your own future manifests itself before you. Indeed, what a glorious thing it is to possess the capacity and ability to think in such a clear and pristine manner. This is when you know you are having a wow moment. This is when you can fully experience the rhythm of life.

As I continued my drive that morning and got closer to my place of work, I merged into the intersection of the dominating highway. I could feel and hear the whining of the tires on the road in conjunction with the music playing from the speakers, as well as the traffic flowing in on the left and on the right, sandwiching me in the middle. It was a drive I was accustomed to, and yet that sudden awareness was acutely there as I maintained my measured mindset to ensure that safety dominated my thinking.

Perhaps one of the things about that particular drive that I've experienced numerous times is how when you're on your game and know you're on your game as you are driving, it's almost like it's just you and the universe. The universe knows exactly what you are about; it knows your heart, it knows your plans, and it synchronizes itself with your intent. Everything falls significantly and purposefully into place, and as that happens, every green light meshes perfectly with your intent. You can drive completely through an entire town and not hit one red light. If you have ever had that experience, then you know exactly what I am talking about.

When life is happening like that for you, those are the best moments, because those are the unstoppable moments. Whatever it is you are thinking about during those moments, you need to capitalize on your thought process. This is when your creativity is at its height; this is when your best inspiration can come. This is when the germination of a new idea can take you to the pinnacle of your success. As these ideas flow through your mind, take the time to capture their essence, write them down, and speak them into a recorder. You are experiencing the rhythm and the flow of a miraculous life. This is truly a powerful thing. You don't have to be in a car when it happens; you can be anywhere. Do you know how many multimillion-dollar ideas were probably written on the backs of napkins when people were sitting in a restaurant and creativity happened to strike? I don't know either. But what I *do* know is this: when creativity strikes, you can feel it, and you know what it is. You simply have to be prepared to capitalize on the new idea, the new approach, or a way of doing things you hadn't quite thought of before.

The rhythm of life enables you to get powerful and amazing things accomplished. All you really have to do is be aware of its existence and be prepared to use it when it comes. Alexander Graham Bell said, "What this power is, I cannot say. All I know is that it exists and it becomes available only when a man or a woman is in that state of mind where he or she knows exactly what he or she wants and is fully determined not to quit until he or she finds it."

Maximize Your Potential

The potential for greatness is awesome.
Acknowledge the spirit within.
Contemplate thoughts of abundance,
True wisdom for women and men.

What is it you wish to attract?
How strong will you try to compete?
How we answer the questions above
Are the things that will make us complete.

The manner in which you approach
Life's virulent obstacle course
Is the one that God will promote
And will help you to fully endorse.

So carefully choose what you read.
Learn from life's challenging tests.
Reject insensitive feedback.
Strive daily to give life your best.

Maximize your potential for greatness.
Press on to reach higher still.
Transcend the limits of others
By engaging your powerful will.

For the power of God is unlimited,
When fully revealed conquers all.
To employ your all powerful ally,
Just stand up and answer the call.

Maximizing Your Potential

Think big and don't listen to people who tell you it can't be done. Life's too short to think small.
—*Tim Ferriss*

This book is replete with an abundance of empowerment materials. Each chapter addresses a particular concept or value in a slightly different way. Perhaps one of the most inspirational awakenings or insights occurs when you discover or read something in a slightly different way than you've even seen it written before. Perhaps the truth of a particular phrase, witty aphorism, or expression causes you to think in a way you've never thought before, and because of that, you are able to connect all of the dots linked to your significant purpose. You become more motivated to fulfill your dreams than you've ever been before.

This internal step toward greatness is indeed a powerful thing. Greatness has many attributes; there isn't just one necessary and essential quality that it must have to secure its place on the mantel above all others.

When I was teaching English at Georgetown Jr. Sr. High School, I had the esteemed honor and privilege of teaching an honors English course. This course encompassed the best and brightest students in the education system. It was a pleasure to have had an opportunity to teach such an outstanding group of future leaders.

We were covering the genre of poetry. I enjoy teaching by theme, and on that particular day, I had incorporated some of the best success-oriented literature in my lecture. I've enjoyed doing this over the years because I know from former graduates that many of these lessons left a significant and lasting impression upon the minds of students. You never know when one word, one poem, or one event will be powerful enough to change someone's life forever. That is what it's all about.

As we were about to open the unit on poetry, I laid down the gauntlet and issued a challenge to my students. I reached in my wallet and pulled out a concise, clean, crisp twenty-dollar bill. I calmly remarked, "Everyone see this twenty-dollar bill?" The room grew quiet, and everyone acknowledged it. "Good," I said. "Today we are going to start a unit on poetry, and I am going to recite a poem. The first person who can tell me the title of this poem or the author who wrote it gets this bill. Are you ready?" All acknowledged, and so I began. "If you can keep your head when all about you are …"

Before I could get any farther, a young lady in the front row by the name of Courtney Mason said, "Dr. Lawson, the name of that poem is 'If,' and the author is Rudyard Kipling." Even though I wasn't completely stunned, I was highly impressed that Courtney knew the answer. Needless to say, I learned a great lesson that day: not to give away twenty-dollar bills anymore—at least, not like that! Since the day Courtney nailed me on that one, I've been a bit more cautious with my poetic assertions. As it turns out, not only is "If" one of my favorite poems, but it was also one of Courtney's.

The point is this that maximizing your potential requires a tremendous amount of balance, precision, and focus, as well as an amazing ability to navigate both turbulence and calm when it comes to life matters. You can count on a certain amount of quietude in your life that will suddenly be interrupted by chaos and events over which you have no control. How well you are able to adjust to and manage those will play a major role in whether or not you will ever develop the ability and the skill to maximize your potential.

All of us are going to be confronted with a series of vicissitudes in life. Yes, there are going to be some good times, but there are going to be bad times too. Rudyard Kipling's powerful and insightful poem hits the nail squarely on the head. The words in this poem are encouraging and thought provoking. Most important, his words tell us precisely how we need to navigate each step of life's journey. The word "if" is a powerful word because it is conditional.

Have you ever thought about the fact that "if" appears right in the center of the word life? It's something to think about.

"If" is the thing that stops most people dead in their tracks. Most people in life cannot get beyond that word. I believe that is one of the primary reasons why Kipling wrote "If" in the first place. He had this innate desire to send a message to the masses of people around the world in order to help them realize that if they're ever going to maximize their potential, the words penned in this poem forever reverberate from heart to heart and from mind to mind, down through the very annals of time as a powerful, resilient truth that is necessary to be reckoned with.

Through his poem "If," Rudyard Kipling leaves with each of us one of life's most powerful and enduring lessons. He wanted people to not only have hope but also to be inspired by hope. His message is permanently and intrinsically linked to the very substance of Emily Dickinson's masterful quote, "Hope is the thing with feathers that perches in the soul and sings the tune without the words and never stops at all." This was indeed the profound depths of Kipling's intellectual imagination and prowess at work.

Obvious points that the poem intimates are a clear indication that Kipling, like most individuals, hadn't gotten through life and achieved anything of imminent significance unblemished and unscathed himself. His powerful poem is a thumbnail sketch that we can all learn deeply from if we take the time to apply the message that this so strongly conveys. If each one of us can do this, then I truly believe that each one of us can maximize the potential we have to achieve greatness. Here is Kipling's poem.

If

If you can keep your head when all about you,
Are losing theirs and blaming it on you;
If you can trust yourself when all men doubt you,
But make allowance for their doubting too.

If you can wait and not be tired by waiting,
or being lied about don't deal in lies,
or being hated don't give way to hating,
And yet don't look to good nor talk to wise.

If you can dream and not make dreams your master,
If you can think and not make thoughts your aim.
If you can meet with triumph and disaster,
And treat those two imposters just the same.

If you can bear to hear the truth you've spoken,
Twisted by knaves to make a trap for fools;
If you can bear to see the things you gave your life to broken.
And stoop and build them up again with worn out tools.

If you can make one heap of all your earnings,
And risk it on one turn of pitch and toss;
And lose and start again at your beginnings,
And never breathe a word about your loss.

If you can force your heart and nerve sinew,
To serve your turn long after they are gone;
If you can still hold on when there is nothing in you,
Except the will which says to them, hold on.

If you can talk with crowds and keep your virtue,
Or walk with kings nor lose the common touch,
If neither foes nor loving friends can hurt you
If all folks count with you but none too much.

If you can fill the unforgiving minute,
With sixty seconds worth of distance run,
Yours is the earth and everything that's in it
And which is more, you'll be a man my son.

Wow! What an incredibly powerful and insightful message on how we should try as hard as possible to live life every single day. There's a balance that each of us must strive to achieve. It's not easy, but it is possible.

A good friend and professional colleague of mine, Dennis Fravel, used to say often when he was teaching across the hall from me, "If ifs and buts were candy and nuts, we'd all have a Merry Christmas." Well, ifs and buts are not candy and nuts.

When we look even deeper into Kipling's powerful poem, we should be able to pinpoint how the concept of greatness runs from heart to heart, spanning every time period known to man. In Dr. Wayne Dyer's book *Inspiration Your Ultimate Calling,* he says, "You must learn to trust yourself when others doubt you." The concept of doubt stymies us all at given periods of our lives. Doubt is the creature that robs us, keeps us poor, and keeps us from maximizing our potential for greatness. Here's what Shakespeare had to say about it: "Our doubts are traitors and make us lose the good we oft might win by fearing to attempt." Don't be averse to stepping out of your comfort zone and trying something completely different.

Again, what a powerful revelation to our hearts, minds, and souls. If we are to be successful in life, we must learn to erase doubt from our thinking. As Dyer mentions in many of his books, we have to move from the realm of believing to the realm of knowing, where doubt is nonexistent. You get to a point in your life where you simply say, "I know I can do it because I just got through doing it." Therein lies the best example of success and the absolute best motivational force in the world and obviously, the one most equipped to deliver the opportunity for one to truly and unequivocally maximize one's potential for greatness.

Enthusiasm Ignites Greatness

Enthusiasm releases the drive to carry you over
obstacles and adds significance to all you do.
—Dr. Norman Vincent Peale

My favorite writer, Ralph Waldo Emerson, once made this profound statement: "Nothing great was even accomplished without enthusiasm." It is my belief that enthusiasm ignites greatness. When you believe 100 percent in something you are doing, there's no question that the exuberance and passion you have for what you are doing will be directly reflected in your work.

Those individuals who come in direct contact with you will get caught up in that aura of excitement that exudes from the inner depths of your soul, when you are immensely on fire for something because you've eradicated all doubt about whether or not it works. The effervescent radiance and exuberance fires your soul in such a manner that it becomes contagious to the majority of those who are in your presence.

There's evidence of it in the teaching profession as well. I believe that students learn best from those individuals who not only have a deep and profound knowledge of the subject matter but also transfer that learning through passion and excitement.

I saw it firsthand in the personalities of Chad McKibben, Holly Woodruff, Mike Jennings, John Copas, and Superintendent Chris Burrows when I worked at Georgetown Jr.-Sr. High School in Georgetown, Ohio. As I made the transition to Chillicothe High School in Chillicothe, Ohio, I witnessed the same kind of exuberance in Teacher of the Year Dustin Weaver, Zach Graves, Barbara Coulter, Greg Phillips, Superintendent Jon Saxton, my former principals Perianne Germann and Jerry Underwood, and my current principal, Dr. Jeffrey Fisher, who is a master teacher, mentor, and friend. These individuals know both the art and science of teaching from the inside out.

One of my profound role models throughout the years has been professional speaker and author Zig Ziglar. Many times I've had the fortunate pleasure of being in the audience and watching his performance up close and personal. One thing that gives me a distinct advantage over many others is my personal knowledge base not only of those astute and savvy individuals, but also due to the fact I've read many of their works and listened to their programs on tape.

Because of that, my mind is saturated to the brim and filled almost to capacity with many of their profound ideas. That is precisely why I can quote verbatim on many of their principles. The primary reason why I've put them to memory is because I know how powerful they are, because they work.

Most of the time when people in my workshops ask me how they can obtain that information, my desire is to give it to them at that moment. If they are in my presence, that is when I can share it with them. Sometimes the knowledge is so great that I cannot wait; people need to have it right now so they can put it to immediate use. That is what I want. I want people to feel the power and feel the sense of urgency so that they can put the knowledge to use right now. The beauty of my taking the time to saturate my mind and immerse myself in the teachings and philosophies of those individuals who are eminent scholars enables me to pay it forward by sharing with others what it takes to achieve levels of unparalleled success.

It pays off handsomely for me because of the profound impact these teachings have had upon my life. In fact, one of the specific phrases that I can recall Zig Ziglar saying that is resounding in my ears as I am writing: "Man was designed for accomplishment, engineered for success and endowed with the seeds of greatness." I have had the opportunity to meet Zig Ziglar personally. I have personal letters that I have received from him in my home. How could I not be impacted in a positive way by those most powerful words? How could I not believe them? You cannot tell me that enthusiasm does not ignite greatness, because it does. Through his books, writings, teachings, and lectures, Zig Ziglar has been one of the most powerful influences this society has ever known. The legacy this great motivator has left behind for millions of individuals to follow will endure forever.

Can you imagine what it is like to receive words of encouragement from one of your greatest mentors? Zig Ziglar was an internationally known personality who had achieved celebrity status, and yet he was selfless in his attitude and actions. It's one of the qualities he had that separated him from the masses of individuals who desired to be like him but would never come close. There was only one original Zig Ziglar. There will never be another. He was a true original. I'm going to share with you brief excerpts from two letters that Zig Ziglar sent me. The first is dated October 3, 1996 and the second is dated October 16, 1996.

Dear Bob,

Thanks for your note. It's an encouragement to me to know my work influenced you to commit yourself to the field of professional public speaking and training. As you have no doubt discovered, Bob, there is today a great need in our society for messages which are pure, clean, powerful, positive and motivating, and it pleases me to know you have joined the ranks of those who are attempting to deliver those messages.

Zig Ziglar

Dear Bob,

Thank you for the autographed and inscribed copy of your book. I appreciate more than you can know being listed among the people who have had a major impact upon your life. It's clear to see that you are using that which you have gained from others to pass on to those who are now coming after. I commend you for that insight and maturity. Bob keep up the great work!

Zig Ziglar

Wow! Words of encouragement from one of the best in the world! How could anyone reflect on these profound words of wisdom and not be inspired? Can you think of someone who has influenced your life in such a powerful manner? Have you figured out a way to let the person know? Perhaps one of those ways would be in preserving a legacy by pouring into individuals whom you meet along life's journey, in the exact same way these individuals poured into you. Remember that enthusiasm ignites greatness.

Because of my associations with profound authors, philosophers, trainers, and speakers of the highest caliber, my own personal and professional growth has benefited substantially. It is no different for you or anyone else who aspires to be a great actor or follow some other passionate endeavor.

Perhaps you choose a budding career in acting, go to Hollywood, and rub shoulders with a few of your show business idols. Finally you meet someone like Tom Hanks, Clint Eastwood, Jodie Foster, Denzel Washington, Meryl Streep, or Oprah Winfrey. You get excited about being around someone you've dreamed about and admired from a distance for years. All that you are now experiencing takes inspiration to a whole new level.

It has been no different for me in the speaking and teaching arena. I have come face-to-face with individuals who specialize in changing lives for the better. I've come to realize and fully appreciate that for me personally, it has been one of life's greatest blessings. I am indeed most grateful for these incredible learning opportunities. Coming face-to-face with Og Mandino, Les Brown, Harvey Alston, Mark Anthony Garrett, Harvey McKay, Patricia Fripp, Zig Ziglar, Jack Canfield, Mark Victor Hansen, and perhaps the greatest mentor and friend I've ever had, Dr. Jeffrey Fisher, who single-handedly helped me achieve the highest possible effective rating a teacher could achieve. His deep and insightful observations, his keen awareness of what must happen in a classroom, and his ability to assist me in shoring up my weaknesses for improvement on a consistent basis are unmatched, equaled only by his desire to see his staff operate at a level of excellence that equals or exceeds all others.

Any time you have the fortunate opportunity to be operating in an arena where the stakes are so high, it forces you to take your game to another level. What you become increasingly aware of is this that when you get close to greatness, it has a significantly positive impact upon your mental psyche. It makes you feel that you too can become great. It lets you know that you haven't yet maximized your potential. You realize that you still have a tremendous opportunity for even more growth, development, and refinement, and that you haven't arrived yet. It also helps you to realize that you too can become great! For you, this becomes one of those exhilarating wow moments.

Any individual whom you encounter who has a positive message that speaks peace to your soul and would never diminish your stature in public or private is someone whom you can greatly admire, appreciate, and benefit from. These people have that spiritual sagacity that encompasses every aspect of their being. It is powerful and real, and it's the primary reason for their success. Again, it was the great Ralph Waldo Emerson who once said, "Greater are they who are able to see that spiritual is stronger than any material force. Thoughts rule the world."

Zig Ziglar explained that enthusiasm comes from the Greek word *entheos*, and the literal translation means "God within." If you look at the last four letters of *enthusiasm*, they could form an acrostic that symbolizes "I Am Sold Myself." Perhaps there is no better way to convince others about what you believe than if you are sold on it yourself.

Indeed, if there is a legacy that I have a desire to leave others, then it would be much the same as many of the great predecessors whom I have aspired to be like over the years. If your desire is strong enough, you have a definite purpose or aim, and you have the ability to keep after it and to not permit others to detract you from your goal—or even if you get sidetracked, you can get started again—then there's no reason why enthusiasm can't ignite greatness.

After all, it is exactly as Zig Ziglar has said: "Other people can only stop you temporarily. You are the only one who can do it permanently."

Thomas Edison had this to say about enthusiasm.

> Enthusiasm goes beyond wealth. It is a zeal for living. It is the force within you that prods you to do your best. It is the expression of dynamic vitality. It's the sparkle in your eye, the eagerness in your voice and the firmness in your

handshake. It's in the way you walk, the way you talk. It's the power that is released to support your definiteness of purpose. It's that quality that kindles a fire under your chief aim and turns it into a burning desire.

It's in the way you walk, the way you talk, and the way you act. It's the result of your physical magnetism and energy. It's the power that is released to support your definiteness of your purpose. It's the spark that kindles a fire under your chief aim and turns it into a burning desire.

Integrity

Integrity is the essence of everything successful.
—R. Buckminster Fuller

Of all the chapters in this book, this is the one that I've been most afraid to write. I've thought long and hard about integrity. It's not difficult to write about concepts and ideas that you know will help people move ahead in life, but it's so much tougher when you have to reveal the shortcomings in your character that you didn't want others to know.

Here's the honest truth. I wish I were perfect, but unfortunately I am not. I have failed so many times in my life. I have made one mistake after another, but for whatever reason God has permitted me to keep striving. In the midst of all my mistakes and failures, I keep getting up and keep trying to get better.

Integrity forces you to take a deep look at who you really are, and it measures you against the person you would like to become. If you are honest with yourself, it reveals all of your flaws and shortcomings. Not all of it's pretty. In fact, it can be downright ugly. It affects how other people feel and think about you, and perhaps even more important, it affects how you think and feel about yourself.

I debated for several years whether or not I would even write this chapter. In the end, I knew that a book like this simply had to have a chapter included on integrity; otherwise, it would not be complete. Besides, if other people had all of the other ingredients they needed to achieve high level success, but they discovered they had no integrity, could they really be considered successful? The answer is no.

Integrity is what holds the mirror up to you and shows you your own reflection. It points the finger at you on a daily basis and says, "I know who you want to be, but who you are and what you do is stopping you from who you can become." It's a tough pill to swallow, but the fact of the matter is that in order to grow, we have to reflect intently on our weaknesses and acknowledge them. Instead of blaming others for our current level of stagnation, we must forgive ourselves for our human frailties.

In James Allen's masterful book *As a Man Thinketh*, he said,

> Before we can achieve anything, even in worldly things, we must lift our thoughts above slavish animal Indulgence, we may not, in order to succeed, all animality and selfishness by any means but a portion of it must, at least be sacrificed. If our first thought is bestial indulgence, we can neither think clearly nor plan methodically; we cannot find and develop our latent resources and would fail in any undertaking. Unless we can strongly control our thoughts, we are not in a position to control affairs and to adopt serious responsibilities. We are not fit to act

independently and stand alone but are limited only by the thoughts which we choose.

There can be no progress, no achievement, without sacrifice, and our worldly success will be in the measure that we sacrifice our confused animal thoughts and fix our mind on the development of our plans and the strengthening of our own resolution and self-reliance. And the higher we lift our thoughts, the more upright and righteous we become, the greater will be our success, the more blessed and enduring will be our achievements.

According to *Webster's New World Dictionary, integrity* is defined as "completeness, unimpaired conditions, soundness, honesty, and sincerity." Perhaps when one examines the word closely, one can catch a glimpse of what Christ meant when he said, "Wilt thou be made whole?"

An individual's integrity serves as the catalystic compass capable of measuring one's true level of greatness. There are so many individuals in our society who have a desire to achieve illimitable measures of success, and yet they find themselves vacillating back and forth in life, hiding under the veil of deception, searching for lasting fame, and achieving what looks like success in the eyes of the public only to fall back into depravity. They are captives to self-imposed limitations because they subject themselves to their pet vices, which serve to inhibit their progress because their integrity is not fully formed. I am one of those people. However, God is not through with me yet. It is much as Brian Tracy has said: "Integrity is more than a value. It is the value that guarantees all other values."

You could say that integrity is the heart and soul of your success. It is the intrinsic merit that penetrates the very fabric of your being. It is in fact the very essence of who you are, how you walk on a daily basis, and what you say. I have discovered that I have to be very careful about what I say and what I write, because on many occasions my words have come back to haunt me. I have discovered that what I have said in the past can resurface in the future and impugn my character in a deleterious manner. I implore you to not let this happen to you. Don't simply trust people on a whim. Get to know them. When you put something in writing to another person, keep in mind that if that individual goes into a fit of rage of anger when the relationship sours, the person can and will use that against you. You should never make that mistake. I have already made it for you.

Integrity is an incredibly powerful attribute. In their book *The Power of Focus*, Mark Victor Hansen and Lleyton Hewitt stated,

> According to 1,300 senior executives who responded to a recent survey, integrity is the human quality most necessary to business success. Seventy-one percent put it at the top of a list of sixteen traits responsible for enhancing an executive's effectiveness.

If you cannot look at yourself in the mirror and be honest with who and what you are in spite of all of your shortcomings, then the real question is, How can you be honest with other people? Integrity starts at home. I know for a fact that my biggest life challenge still lies in front of me. I know that try as I might, I am still an imperfect human being, and yet I acknowledge that fact. Each day that I am able to get up, I'm going to try to be a little bit better than I was the day before. And though there will be days that I am unable to accomplish that objective, I am never going to give up on myself. If I did that, I would never be able to encourage others to reach for the dreams and goals they have set for themselves. I want people to realize their dreams and ambitions. My ultimate purpose in life lies in encouraging them to do so. Still, sometimes, it is hard to do when you have failed to live up to the standards and expectations you have set for yourself.

Setting the example by what you do is a far greater testimony to success than what you talk about. The old adage "I'd rather see a sermon any day than hear one" is quite true.

Anytime I hear the word *integrity*, I'm reminded of the powerful poem "The Man in the Glass" by Dale Wimbrow. It stands as a symbol for all of society, and it's a powerful reminder to each of us to "work from where we are with what we have until we get to where we want to be." Here it is.

The Man in the Glass

When you get what you want in your struggle for self,
And the world makes you king for a day;
Just go to a mirror and look at yourself,
And see what that man has to say.

You may fool the whole world on the pathway of life,
And get pats on your back as you pass;
But your final reward will be heartaches and tears,
If you've cheated the man in the glass.

It is my hope that you have found this chapter insightful, motivational, and inspirational. As my friend and colleague Gene Murphy and I watched the Cleveland Cavaliers annihilate the Golden State Warriors by setting an all-time record for the number of points scored in the first quarter of an NBA Finals game (49) in 2017, the record they beat was set in 1982, when the Lakers played the Boston Celtics, Gene texted me a quote that I want to share with you. These players are the elite of the elites, and even though most in our society will become more successful in life by getting regular jobs and keeping them (because most professional ballplayers 78 percent will wind up bankrupt when they reach retirement age), stars like LeBron James, Stephen Curry, Kyrie Irving are exceptions to the rule. Consider this integrity issue. This is what my friend has said, and each of us would perhaps be a small bit wiser if we reflected on his powerful words of growth and insightful encouragement.

When you get to the top of your profession, no one can destroy you but yourself. These guys can pay all their bills, plus travel the world and live a life unimaginable to the masses. The only losers are those who are postponing their own dreams as they sleepwalk through life.

The Power of Choice

We design our lives through the power of choices.
—Richard Bach

The choices you make in life are ultimately what make you. It is as the great seventeenth-century philosopher John Locke said: "The mind is a blank tablet on which true experience shall write." Perhaps we should be the ones who see to it that those experiences are ones that our offspring will be proud of. Our life experiences determine who we are, and we can influence the opportunity for those experiences to be positive simply by the life choices we make.

These ideas are not new. They've been around since the beginning of time and commenced with Adam and Eve's fall in the Garden of Eden.

The power of choice is a very evident and obvious principle at work in the lives of each and every one of us on a daily basis.

Your destiny does not have to be what other people say it will be. You do not have to follow in the footsteps of those who have preceded you, particularly if theirs is a legacy of pain, guilt, irreverence, and shame. You can overcome all of that. I have been guilty of making some very sad and stupid mistakes. The good news is that I don't have to keep making them.

Every day when our alarm clock goes off, motivational speaker Zig Ziglar refers to it as an opportunity clock. The sum total of our thoughts and our experiences are right there with us as we get out of bed and greet the new day. It is much as William Jennings Bryan has said: "Destiny is not a matter of chance. It is a matter of choice. It is not a thing to be hoped for. It is a thing to be achieved." These are powerful words indeed, and hopefully the truth that lies in the essence of this quote will resonate with our spirits in such a quixotic and esoteric fashion that we will be inspired to act on a particular purpose or cause that seeks to build a successful and positive societal order—and one that is constructively designed to benefit others.

If our minds are filled with constructive thoughts and ideas, this increases the opportunity for us to make wise choices. In order to become more successful in our ventures, we can apply these concepts to every individual facet of our lives. The majority of the life choices that you make today will do one of two things. They will reward you in ways that you could never have imagined possible, or they may serve to detract from your person in a very negative way.

It is as Brian Tracy said in his *Book of Wisdom*: "You are always free to choose what you do less of, and what you do not at all." The other thing that we must consider is that the choices we make don't impact just us— they impact everyone around us. It takes a very long time for us to grow out of being selfish and realize that decisions that we make affect not only the quality of our lives but the quality of the lives of others as well.

Many people live a lifetime without maturing to the point where they realize how the decisions they've made affect others. Let me share a personal story in an attempt to illustrate how the choices you make in life can help you to move in a certain direction.

A number of years ago, I was inspired to write a book. Its title was *Destined for Greatness*. Because of the book's content, which focused on both personal and professional empowerment strategies through goal setting, leadership, organizational development, motivation, and more, I became fairly well-known as a seminar and keynote presenter for many state-level organizations. There are eighty-eight counties in the state of Ohio. I remember specifically going to Brown County. I had been hired to conduct a three-day retreat for a teacher in-service event. Instructors were about to return to the classroom for another full year.

I had done extensive research and invested a lot of time, energy, and effort in order to help teachers gear up for another year in the classroom. There were a couple hundred instructors involved because this was a district-wide program. When I finished, the seminar reviews from participants were excellent.

The following year, when summer rolled around, I received a call from Jim Frazer, who was serving as assistant superintendent down in Brown County at that time. Jim had played a significant role in my being invited to present in Brown County in the first place. Jim hadn't purchased my book, *Destined for Greatness,* in a bookstore. That would have cost him $16.95. He was browsing in a goodwill store one day and found a copy of it for twenty-five cents! He noticed at the time that I worked full time at Shawnee State University in Portsmouth, Ohio, as the director of continuing education. What intrigued him most was that he had a daughter who had attended there. Jim was fascinated with the book, read the entire thing, and sent me an e-mail to see if I was the guy who had written the book. One thing led to another, and that's how this whole process got started.

When Jim called the following year, this was to be an in-service program for seventy to eighty administrative personnel. Jim remembered how well my previous program had been received, and he wanted to know what my fee would be to conduct the annual retreat, which was to be held at the Shawnee State Park Lodge. Ironically, it was a stone's throw from my house.

As a result of several conversations, we reached a satisfactory agreement for all parties involved, but it only gets better from here. The first day, when I walked in to conduct the workshop, I was dressed, pressed, and looking my best.

My good friend Harvey Alston once told me, "Image is everything." Another good friend of mine, whom I hadn't seen in years, placed his finger in the center of my back. We had graduated from high school together. His name was Mike Fadeley, and Mike just happened to be the guidance counselor at Georgetown, Jr.-Sr. High School in Brown County, Ohio. Later that evening, Mike introduced me to the principal, Perianne Germann, and to the assistant principal, Greg Barlow. We had a great time conversing about a number of things.

The following day, I began facilitation of the workshop on leadership development and training. I spent an abundant amount of time interacting with my professional colleagues and peers.

Superintendent Mike Smith was in attendance as well. Earlier, he and Perianne had spoken to me about an English vacancy they were in the process of filling. They wanted to know if I was available to consider it. My friend Mike Fadeley had also put in a good word on my behalf.

I made the decision to come home and follow up with the principal and superintendent by writing a letter of interest, in which I shared my extensive background and training, strengths, and skills. After several discussions with administrators, I was made an offer commensurate with my background and experience. I took the matter to the board of education for approval and wound up teaching for a nine-year period in the Georgetown Jr.-Sr. Exempted Village High School system.

My purpose for sharing that story is to illustrate how the choices you make can significantly impact where you wind up in life. As you review with some interest what my personal decisions were, I'm more hopeful that you will reflect upon your own life to see what decisions or changes you can make that will significantly impact your own life in a positive and incredibly powerful way.

- Making the decision to obtain a college degree (Life Choice, or LC)
- Making the decision to obtain an advanced degree (LC)
- Making the decision to obtain a doctoral degree (LC)
- Deciding to write a book (LC)
- Decision to get book published (LC)
- Decision to conduct a professional workshop for teachers
- Decision to conduct workshop for administrative personnel
- Maintain a favorable relationship with Mike Fadeley
- Maintain my state certification in a specialized area
- Having a valid teaching certificate
- Staying drug free

This is just one example of how the choices you make in life can play a significant role in the outcomes. It is not a laughing matter. Life choices are very serious business, and they impact every aspect of your life. All of the other individuals involved in this process had to make decisions as well. They had to consult with one another and make a decision about me, what they perceived about my reputation and my character, and whether or not I was the best person for that job.

That's how it works.

There were physical exams I had to pass, as well as the fingerprint and FBI background check to determine whether or not I had been convicted of a felony. I took a urine analysis to make sure I didn't test positive for the use of illegal drugs or banned substances.

If someone young is reading this chapter on choices, my hope is that you realize now that the choices you make can have a dramatic impact (negative or positive) on your life in later years.

If you have sex prior to marriage, at least consider the consequences. If you commit a burglary or break the law in some other way, consider the consequences. If you are involved in illegal drug use, consider how that is going to affect your life. If you are of a working age and are unemployed, do some self-analysis and consider why that is.

If you are unmotivated to do well in life, and you are playing the blame game and laying all of the guilt at the feet of others or a plethora of reasons, this is a classic case of denial, and you need help. It's the person you see when you look in the mirror. You're refusing the help you need. No one's coming to rescue you. You will have to rescue yourself. If you won't voluntarily seek the professional help and counseling you need to get your life on track, then know now that the alternative choices for you are slim to none: prison or death. If that's how you want it to end, it's your choice.

However, it doesn't have to end there. Whatever your reason is for not living and just barely existing, you can have a change of attitude, a change of heart. If you really want to, you can make the decision to turn things around. You can start taking some responsibility for your own life. Stop whining and blaming others for what has to come from inside of you. You don't really need multiple excuses to not succeed. All you need is one excuse, and you're pretty much done.

What you really need to do is bury your excuses so far deep into the ground that nothing can ever bring them to the surface to haunt you again. From that moment, start owning the power of choice by memorizing and internalizing the powerful words of Theodore Roosevelt.

> Do not choose to be common. It is your right to be uncommon. Seek opportunity to develop whatever talent God gave you, not security. Do not wish to be a kept citizen humbled and dulled by having the state to look after you. Do not barter incentive for a dole. Learn to

take the calculated risk, to dream, and to build, to fail and to succeed. Prefer the challenges of life to guaranteed existence and the thrill of fulfillment to the stale calm of Utopia. Do not trade your freedom for beneficence nor your dignity for a handout. Never cower before any earthly master nor bend to any threat, why? Because it is your heritage to stand erect, proud and unafraid, to think and act yourself. To enjoy the benefits of your creation and to face the world boldly and say, this with God's help I have done. All of this is what it means to be an American.

Habits

You'll never change your life until you change something you do
daily. The secret of your success is found in your daily routine.
—*John C. Maxwell*

I worked as the director of continuing education at Shawnee State University from 1990 to 1997. In early 1990, Dr. Stephen Covey had emerged as one of the top leaders in the country. He had just published his amazing book *The Seven Habits of Highly Effective People*. Soon after, he would follow that up with another powerful book, *The Eighth Habit*. My associate director, Virginia Ramey and I went to Cincinnati to meet Dr. Covey.

Approximately eight hundred people were in attendance at the seminar. It was a powerful and revealing session. Here was an individual with a staff of professionals who had conducted extensive research on the very foundation of all of the principles it took to become successful in life from both a personal and a professional perspective. In his research, Dr. Covey unearthed the base of the tree, if you will allow me to use that as an analogy. He showed readers over the years the role that character plays in establishing a solid foundation based on integrity, which I've already written about. Some of the more modern leaders focused on the personality ethic as opposed to the character ethic. These observations were powerful and revealing.

What is amazing to me is how life works. After sitting through numerous seminars and digesting this valuable information years later, I ran into Dr. Jeffrey Fisler, principal of Chillicothe High School, who hired me to teach juniors and seniors in an effort to help them transition to college. Little did I know at the time that Chillicothe High School in Chillicothe, Ohio, had embraced and adopted the "Leader in Me" system, which was straight out of Dr. Covey's book. Talk about coincidence or luck! To me, it wasn't either. This was a divinely orchestrated event, and it had captured my full attention.

As I walked the halls with administrative officials and interfaced with future colleagues, we stopped in the cafeteria. All over the cafeteria walls, as well as in the hallways, were big, bold, colorful words—the seven habits of highly effective people. Wow! I knew immediately that God had now placed me exactly where he wanted me to be. I needed no training to teach these concepts and ideas to my students because I was already living them daily, and they were deeply engrained in the fabric of my heart. I knew them and the essence of what they stood for verbatim and could discuss them for hours with my students. The habits were an extension of who I was. I had read both of Dr. Covey's books and had been practicing his philosophy of life ideas for several years before arriving at Chillicothe High School. I had also read his books *Principle Centered Leadership* and *Putting First Things First*.

If you desire to dig deeper into Dr. Covey's work to fully understand

and apply the intrinsic merit of what he has discovered, I strongly urge and encourage you to do so. The more knowledgeable you become, the more you will be able to apply what you have learned to become even more effective as a person and as a leader.

To help you more clearly understand the nature of daily living and the principles of leadership, it is essential for us to understand how we are to utilize the tools we are given. The more we understand how to use what is given to us, the more effective we can be, and the greater will be our results.

For example, which has more power and resolve in the heart of a mighty storm? Is it the mighty oak that tends to stand strong, rigid, and firm when the mighty winds of the hurricane or the tornado sweep through? Or is it the weeping willow that bends when the breath of the mighty wind seeks to uproot it from the ground? At times, it is bold and intrepid strength that has high merit because it resists all pressure to conform, and at other times it is those who understand the nature of the storm and demonstrate flexibility who are the survivors and live to fight another day. What a powerful lesson for those who seek to keep moving forward and upward in life.

Dr. Covey's powerful book discusses at great length the seven habits by being proactive. Begin with the end in mind. Put first things first, think win-win, seek first to understand and then to be understood, and sharpen the saw and synergy.

He provides his readers with an in-depth analysis of how each one of these key principles work in an effort to assist individuals in developing a powerful, interdependent nature regarding their interactions with one another, as well as how each habit can be applied specifically to one's life to enhance its effectiveness even further.

There has never been any doubt that the burgeoning success factor in all great achievement is linked directly to the formation of good habits. What is a habit, anyhow? It is a thing that gets repeated over and over until it becomes ingrained in the subconscious mind and operates as an unconscious action that an individual begins to perform with relative ease.

Habits can be negative or positive. Those that become an integral part of who we are early in our lives will either serve us well or wind up making us their servants. Perhaps nothing can be worse than becoming a slave to a habit that has no positive purpose or meaning.

In order to discover what is preventing you from arriving at the destination you desire, you must examine yourself, analyze and identity the behaviors that are prohibiting your progress, and make a conscientious effort to replace them with more desirable habits. Even though this is easier said than done, it is still quite possible. It requires a daily honest assessment of the self. It requires you asking yourself questions like, "What is preventing me from getting where I'd like to be? What am I willing to do about it?" That bit of information is the bottom line. Continue to pose questions for yourself carefully. "What is my environment like? Who am I being influenced by? How am I benefiting from the influence? How am I not benefiting? Is the influence positive or negative? What habits of thought and action do I have, and what must I do to change them if they are not positive?" The first step lies in your ability to be honest with yourself. Without self-integrity, there is no future hope.

You set yourself up for success by the very creation of an environment that is conducive to the cultivating and bringing out of your greatest talents and skills. The old adage "Sow a thought, reap an act, sow an act, reap a habit, sow a habit, reap a character and sow a character, reap a destiny" is very accurate.

Let's start at the root of a problem—in this case, a thought. If that thought is a negative and debilitating thought that does no one any earthly good, we can uproot that thought upon inception and replace it with something meaningful and good. Considering the fact that thoughts have energy, they can empower you or make you feel helpless and disenfranchised. Even the thoughts of others can impact you a certain way. Whether a thought is good or bad, people have a general tendency to act on what they spend time thinking about. What starts out as a thought becomes an action, and if that action begins to occur in a repeated fashion, it crystallizes into a habit. That habit begins the formation of true character.

For example, if we lie repeatedly, soon it becomes second nature. If we steal, it becomes second nature, and we become callous to it; it becomes a way of life. If, on the other hand, we encourage positive behaviors in ourselves, these positive behaviors will tend to yield positive results. Whatever it is that becomes the ultimate focus or intent of your mind is what gets accomplished. Thoughts determine the majority of the outcomes in your life. This is precisely why the formation of good habits is so powerful.

In William James Tilley's 1889 edition of his incredible book *Masters of the Situation*, you will find these words penned exactly as they were stated in the chapter on habits.

> Every man carries within himself to a great extent his own destiny – undaunted will, unflinching energy, ever and everywhere make their mark and bring success. In business, who is the man that succeeds? The man who thinks clearly, plans wisely and executes promptly and with untiring energy.

Many persons wonder why men of great fortune continue to labor, instead of resting and enjoying themselves, and attribute it to mere love of gain. They forget that long habit becomes second nature, that such men find rest in constant occupation, and that enjoyment prescribed for them would be the severest form of punishment that could be inflicted.

Habit thus becomes destiny. "God gives us the power to form habits that we may crystallize victories. All improvement in the eye of the painter, in the tongue of the orator, in the hand of the artisan, is the gift of habit. It is a channel worn in the substance of the soul, along which our purpose and our ability to run with increased facility. The formation of a habit reduces to this single direction. Apply yourself to any course marked out for yourself industriously, punctually, and persistently, and you prevail. You have this marvelous power at command—use it.

In Dr. Stephen Covey's book *The Eighth Habit*, there's a powerful passage by an anonymous writer.

> I am your constant companion. I am your greatest helper or heaviest burden. I will push you onward or drag you down to failure. I am completely at your command. Half the things you do you might just as well turn over to me, and I will be able to do them quickly, correctly. I am easily managed, you must merely be firm with me. Show me exactly how you want something done, and after a few lessons I will do it automatically. I am the servant of all great people; and alas, of all failures as well. Those who are failures, I have made failures. I am not a machine, though I work with all the precision of a machine plus the intelligence of a human being. You may run me for a profit or turn me for ruin – it makes no difference to me. Take me, train me, be firm with me, and I will place the world at your feet. Be easy with me and I will destroy you. Who Am I? I am habit.

In closing this chapter, one of Dr. Covey's most profound discoveries that staggered him to his core is one that everyone should have an opportunity to see. Here it is.

> Between stimulus and response there is a space. In that space lies our freedom and power to choose our response. In those choices lie our growth and happiness.

Book II

Resilience

There is no value judgment more important to an individual;
no factor more decisive in his psychological development and
motivation than the estimate he places upon himself.
—Nathaniel Branden

Resilience is a quality that every individual who desires to achieve great success must have. In order to achieve great success, you must equip yourself to handle the various adversities with which you will be confronted. It is as Mattison has said: "Those who have not failed will not have the knowledge they need to move forward." The world is full of examples of individuals who live under the microscope of the media because of their fame. You know all about their indiscretions. The world scrutinizes them mercilessly and will tell them in an instant what they can and cannot do no matter how good they might be.

Whether these individuals have been found guilty or were exonerated because of a lack of evidence, can you imagine the stress and turmoil these individuals and their alleged victims have experienced over the years? Whether it's Tiger Woods, Bill Clinton, Mary K. Letourneau, Paula Dean, Marion Jones, Hillary Clinton, Bill Cosby, Donald J. Trump, or Anthony Wiener, there's always a media frenzy centered on the activities concerning these individuals. When will it ever stop so that we can start focusing on the real issues affecting this country? It probably never will, and for good reason. All of these individuals must be held accountable. To a lesser degree, this also includes us.

The real question for you and me is this: How will we handle our own personal adversity, and how will we respond to the criticism that is leveled at us when things are not going well? There will always be those who are quick to point out your flaws, weak points, and faults. The manner in which you are able to resolve the odds that are stacked against you is something that will help to determine the true measure of your character.

Any individual who has the innate desire to achieve lasting and permanent success must be able to bounce back from low points in life and work hard to surpass where one once was. This astounding resilience requires a natural mindset that is not a part of the general masses of people as we know it. It has much to do with your personal resolve as well as the time, energy, and effort you must spend to regain or exceed your previous level of dominance.

You have to be hard-wired to know yourself and your capabilities better than anyone else. What is it that you demand of yourself? It was Dr. Julius Irving who once said, "I demand more of myself than anyone else could ever expect." Imagine that! I say, imagine that simply because most people can't.

In order to be successful, one must be able to negotiate the vicissitudes of life in an admirable and sustained fashion. Your ability to be resilient is a success attribute that will enable you to dominate your competition and overcome your own self-doubt and limitations.

In order to be resilient and overcome all of the odds that are stacked against you, consider the fact that you only have one earthly life to live. If that is the case, shouldn't you prepare yourself for the fight of your life? No matter what it is that people tell you, no matter what it is they say about you, you should do your very best to continuously be prayerful. While doing so, prepare for the fight of your life every day. Here's a powerful, original poem that I have written that will serve as an encouragement to you while you are on the battlefield, preparing to do what is necessary to achieve your goals.

Dr. Robert L. Lawson

The Fight

"Stop! Stay down! It's over!" They look at me and shout.
But then my mind recalls a fighter's distant bout.
And as I am reminded of that grueling match of wit,
I'm once again encouraged to not give up and quit.

Two heavyweights were vying for the world's prestigious crown.
Each thought that he would win and knock the other down.
Both men were highly confident as they stepped into the ring.
Their entourage had followed them and waited in the wing.

They looked each other up and down, each trying hard to con.
They stared each other eye to eye, and then the fight was on.
Each fighter came out punching hard to try his best to win.
Each fighter popped an uppercut to smash the other's chin.

As the fight drew on and on, 'twas plain for all to see
That the taller of these two big men might gain the victory.
The taller man swung mighty hard, and the shorter man went down.
You could feel the building shake as he hit the ground.

The ref he counted, one, two, three, and he was up again,
Still vying for the title, still thinking he could win.
The taller man hit harder still, the shorter fell again,
And the crowd began to question his ability to win.
The taller man began to shout. "Stay down, stay down," he said.
"I don't want to be the one to break your friggin' head."
But something deep inside of him, in spite of all the pain,
Caused the shorter of these two to rise up once again.

146

The taller man was struck with awe; he couldn't believe his eyes
As the shorter of the two once more began to rise.
The taller hit him once again, and on the mat he went.
This time it looked quite hopeless; his energy was spent.

And as the taller raised his arms to claim the victory,
He heard a buzzing in the room and turned around to see
The shorter man had gotten up, still standing in the ring.
He shook his finger, then he said, "Fat lady did not sing."

The crowd was in a state of shock as the shorter threw a punch.
Connecting with the taller man that ended in a crunch.
The taller fell. The fight was over. It had ended now.
Somewhere the talk continues though of just exactly how.
Sometimes life throws you obstacles; it seems there's no way out.
Sometimes it seems not fair at all; it's like the fighter's bout.
Sometimes you're hit so hard in life, you lose your will to live,
It's at those moments that you find you still have more to give.
He could have quit; he could have lain there thinking, "I've struck out.
I've been knocked down three times today. I can't erase this doubt."

"Stop! Stay down! It's over!" They look at me and shout.
And then my mind recalls a fighter's distant bout.
When others try to steal your dream and break your will to win,
Remember the fighter's distant bout. Rise up and try again.

My hope is that you have found this chapter on resilience refreshing, inspirational, challenging, thought provoking, encouraging, and empowering. Right now, you ought to be feeling like there is nothing that you cannot accomplish. It is never what other people may be thinking, feeling, or saying about you. What should matter to you more than anything else is what you are thinking, feeling, seeing, and believing about yourself. That is the thing that will carry you across the finish line and enable you to do things you've never done before. Resiliency is your ability to get up just one more time than you've been knocked down.

In closing this chapter, let me leave you with these profound and insightful words from my good friend, motivational and empowerment speaker Harvey Alston. "We must be tough enough to fight for what is right; tender enough to care for those who cry out for our help; strong enough to absorb the pain of criticism and failure yet resilient enough to bounce back."

The Battlefield of the Mind

The mind is a terrible thing to waste!
—UNCF slogan

Each person has his or her own opinions and thoughts about things. What one person needs in a given moment may be quite different from what someone else needs. Each chapter in this book is powerful and unique in its own right in terms of its relationship and intent for the reader. This could be one of the most powerful chapters in this book because the essence of your mind is what actually controls every other event in your life. It is as Jim Rohn has said, If we can develop the ability to "stand guard at the door of your mind and control the thoughts as they come in," you can direct yourself to do those things that will enable you to stay focused on what needs to get done instead of meandering all over the place.

The ability to take charge of your life and to stay motivated and focused on your goals consistently is the very thing that will put you over the top. Zig Ziglar used to say in his seminars all the time, "Are you a wandering generality, or are you a meaningful specific?" The first time I heard him say that, I thought it was funny, but the more I thought about it, the more I kept asking myself, "What are you doing with your life? Where are you going? Do you even know?" It was no longer funny—it was serious business.

In my earlier years, *Star Trek* was one of my favorite shows, with William Shatner as Captain Kirk and Leonard Nimoy as his Vulcan sidekick, Spock. "Space, the final frontier. To boldly go where no man has gone before." Really? Is that accurate? Let's analyze this a little bit. How can we conquer outer space when we haven't even conquered inner space? Pause and let that thought sink in for a moment. What would make us think that we can conquer outer space when we haven't even conquered inner space, the six inches between our ears? Before we can think about what we can do out in the far reaches of the universe, shouldn't we figure out how to get control of our own thinking first? Why else would Emerson have ever said, "What lies behind us and what lies before us are tiny matters compared to what lies within us"?

Interpret that however you want, but I think what he was actually saying is that if we can get our minds to stay focused on things that are highly insightful to our growth and development and our creativity as human beings, then there is no limit to what we are capable of accomplishing. We have to force ourselves to stay focused on the important things and stop letting other things detract us from our goals. Those individuals who become the most successful are those who simply refuse to allow the distractions that are in their lives to take over and pull them off task. It's all about how and what you think.

The obtainment of greatness is not going to be something that comes easily. It is a long, arduous, and exceptionally difficult path. It is an incredible process that not many can adhere to. This is why Ecclesiastes 9:11 states, "Again I saw under the sun the race is not to the swift, nor the battle to the strong, nor bread to the wise, nor riches to the intelligent, nor favor to those with knowledge, but time and chance happen to them all."

The obtainment of positive, pure success that is designed to benefit the masses of people requires a strict and tenacious ability to the principles of God's work. God can and will reward those who seek his powerful purpose, which can emanate through their lives.

The first battle that you must overcome is not one that you will encounter in the external world. As you grow, develop, and hopefully learn from your experiences (many people don't), you will discover that your greatest challenges are the obstacles, hurdles, temptations, landmines, and booby traps that permeate the very essence and fabric of your own mind.

In order to be truly successful in life, there are so many desires that you are reluctant to let go of or give up. These are all the things that stand between you and your efforts to get to the doorway of greatness and walk through. God is waiting there for you. He yearns so very much to greet you and smile upon you, with numerous blessings awaiting you and his arms open. He wants to say, "Well done, my good and faithful servant. You have been diligent and faithful over a few things. Now, let me make you a ruler over many."

Oh, if it were so easy! But it is not. The truth of the entire matter is that daily, we sabotage our very own success, and even our own existence, by the poor, pitiful decisions that we make. Yes, every single day we fall victim to our very own fanciful whims, bad habits, cravings for drugs, sexual promiscuity, and addictions that all too often keep us from pursuing those things that are wholesome and would place us at the threshold of greatness. It is truly a sad commentary on the status of the human condition.

It is in our times of weakness that we must cry out to the only one who is truly equipped to come to our aid. If we truly want to be successful in our lives, we must cry out to God when we are in our weakened state and say,

> Father, I have sinned. Please forgive me. With your strength, enable me to overcome my personal weaknesses that are holding me back, so that I may continue to press forward to the mark of the high calling in Christ Jesus. It is you whom I call upon to reject all of those things that are holding me back. Give me the bold and intrepid strength to move forward, grasp your unchanging hand, and power my way victoriously to the front of the line.

The first battle I must win is the one that rages in my own mind. In my human condition, I am sometimes weak and powerless but when I delve into your word and hide its powerful passages within my heart, then I can recall them and act upon them accordingly. Your way is the only clear path to righteous victory and many good works that are capable of benefiting others. This is what I desire to do with my life. It is my very thoughts that will determine my future. The manner in which I move to control them and act upon them that is closest to your will is what will generate the results necessary for the acquisition of success in my life.

A war is raging inside my head, and whether I win or lose the battle against myself is incumbent upon my attitude toward your word and whether or not I will allow it to infiltrate my heart to the point where I will follow your guidance or squander away all that you have given me for something that looks so good on the surface but underneath is deadly and full of dead men's bones. God, help me daily to walk in humility and make these decisions for which I know you will be proud. It is as Anthony Robbins has said: "It is in your moments of decision that your destiny is shaped."

We must control our thoughts. Those thoughts we possess are the backbone of our actions. The actions that we take will lead us to victory or to the pit of self-destruction. Help us to be strong in our decision making by working hard to overcome the weaknesses in our minds that are upon us every waking hour of the day. Help us to overcome those thoughts that seek to render us helpless and powerless, cause us great pain after temporal and ephemeral pleasure, and give us the strength that will empower us to do incredible things. Help us, oh God, every day to sidestep the vicious minefields hidden in the human mind so that we win the battles and the war against spiritual wickedness in high places. Then victory will be yours.

As Susan Taylor said, "Thoughts have energy, thoughts have power and you can make or break your own future by your own thinking." You must work continuously to lift your thoughts to higher levels of comprehension and understanding. The great writer Ralph Waldo Emerson tells us precisely why. "The ancestor of every action is a thought." What we hold firmly in our minds is soon acted upon. It is then incumbent upon each and every one of us to seek internal nobility in our attempt to map our own minds accordingly. It is the roadmap of our minds that determines what it is that we finally act upon in real life. Our ability to raise our thought awareness to a higher level will determine the ultimate quality of our manifested reality. Emerson stated, "I count him a great man who inhabits a higher sphere of thought into which other men rise with labor and difficulty." A preponderance of the evidence would suggest that this keen observation from one of our greatest philosophers is both critical and paramount to a life that aspires itself to be destined for greatness.

The Attitude of Success

Whether or not you think you can or you can't, either way, you are right.
—Henry Ford

Success is a nebulous term that must be defined by each individual. There are many equations that formulate the ideas that drive the concept of success. Success also has an attitude. This attitude is one that displays the quality of high-level confidence, a never-say-die approach to life, infectious and contagious enthusiasm, and a strong desire to continue moving forward in the face of overwhelming opposition. Yes, success has an attitude. It is never an attitude of ambivalence or one that has a tendency to focus on negativity. When you encounter someone who possesses the mentality of a champion, you know it immediately. All of them possess the ability to help you to understand that you too can become great in your particular field of endeavor if you take the time to apply the same success principles to your life that they did. This is the modus operandi of a real winner.

It's not a haughty arrogance that they possess; it's the it factor that the majority of people look for in life but never find. The reason why people never find it is because it remains buried deep inside of them. They never discover it and never develop it because they never take the time to look inward. This is one of the major components for those who are looking to achieve major success in life. Individuals who are highly confident about themselves and their skill sets have the ability to demonstrate active humility through their persona. They have no need to boast about their achievements; their body of work speaks for itself. You will know by their knowledge base, the manner in which they present themselves, and their willingness to provide you with the tools you need to improve your own self-worth. Those are the attributes of successful individuals.

Their attitude is always on display on a daily basis, and most of the time you will find that real winners are consistent. Generally speaking, their walk matches their talk. True champions know that they were put here to serve and to make a positive difference in the lives of others. This is the true attitude of success. It's not that difficult to spot those who are disingenuous; they pretend to care about world problems when others show concern about national issues. It's all for show. Yet they are so busy that they neglect those who are closest to them. Don't let that be you. If you're not sincere, success will be yours but only for a fleeting moment; it cannot last. Those who achieve lasting success are those who have sought and found the true meaning of service. This is the true attitude of success, the measure of greatness, and the heart of a champion.

On this road to greatness, success contains so many variables, and one must figure out effective ways in which they can draw from each of their specific sources of inspiration. As the poem that follows shows, there can be so much wisdom in the statement of a good friend, a good book, a quote, an experience, or something you thought you were doing right. Whatever it is that you can learn from is something that can place you a little closer to the goal you have set for yourself. The things in which you are involved can become a powerful impetus to assist in driving you forward.

Each day, we are blessed to see life unfold and illustrate the lesson it has framed to teach us. The true essence and the attitude of success is this: Nothing in life happens unless you take the initiative to make it happen. You have to be willing to take some risks. In his book *Risking*, Dr. David Viscott says, "If your life is ever going to get better, you've got to take some chances." Upon further reading in Dr. Viscott's book, I came across another quote that could have a profoundly positive impact upon others. It is a quote by the famous Helen Keller. The next time you are further refining and molding your attitude of success, and doubt and fear creep in to sabotage your forward progression, try to remember these great words of wisdom. Perhaps you will feel liberated.

Helen Keller says, "Security is mostly a superstition. It does not exist in nature, nor do the children of men as a whole experience it. Avoiding danger is no safer in the long run than outright exposure. Life is either a daring adventure or nothing."

This is the only way you can move forward. The old adage is quite true: you can't steal second base by keeping your foot on first. Get out there and get started by taking action today.

What Does It Take to Succeed?

Sometimes it takes a powerful quote
To help you understand,
Unravel the mystery of where you are
As you carefully craft your plan.

Sometimes it takes a powerful book
That one must simply read
To take ideas and act on them
And focus on doing a deed.

At other times it takes a friend
To spread a word of cheer
And help you to resolve the things
That hold you back in fear.

Sometimes it takes experience
And challenges to work through,
As you contemplate the strategies
And learn what you must do.

Sometimes it takes adversity
That you must overcome,
And negotiate some failures
Before you've actually won.

You have to be relentless
To understand success.
You have to be tenacious
And strive to be your best.

To understand success,
You have to make a pact.
It's solely with yourself
That you must learn to act.

Introduction II

For almost four decades, I had tried unsuccessfully to write an introduction worthy of consideration for "The Resolution of Perseverance," a writing that God placed in my heart and mind to pen at the age of thirty-six and share with others. Everything that I attempted fell far short of that mark—until I stumbled across Orison Marden's masterfully skilled 1800s book, *Pushing to the Front,* which I discovered at age sixty-seven.

As I delved into his masterful publication, it was there that I was able to ascertain what exactly had happened to me at age thirty-six that, until now, I had been unable to articulate and write about with any sense of clarity to help others comprehend in a forthright manner.

"The Resolution of Perseverance" is easily my greatest contribution to society. I have never written anything of this caliber prior to this publication, and I can almost say with certainty that I never will write something so important again. Of course, that will be left to the judgment of my contemporaries.

Those writers whose pens have fallen under the spell of spiritual guidance will understand when I say that the words you are about to read in this book were placed in my mind by a power far greater than anything I had ever encountered before. I was merely a willing vessel through which the Holy Spirit would work its magnificent and incredible purpose.

When I finished, I can assure you that when I read and reread the manuscript, each time I was dumbfounded and amazed that God had selected me as the vehicle through which he would work his ultimate purpose.

Even today, decades later, when I pick up "The Resolution of Perseverance" and read its deep and amazing content, I am able to see things that I never saw before. I can understand things more clearly than I ever have before. What it says to me in essence is this: "The Resolution of Perseverance" is a living document that will ooze through your every pore, quicken your spirit, and fill it with an abundance of powerful principles to live by.

As I reflect briefly on the mindset I was in at the time of this writing, there are several things about which I want to make you acutely aware. The Bible has served as my guide and source of inspiration for my life. When everyone else has deserted and rejected me and left me to drown in a sea of unbelief, it was and always will be God who picks me up and renders me safely to exactly where it is he decides he wants me to be. He has always made sure that he has duly prepared me for the moment of success that is to arrive at a precise time in my life. I give God total credit for that without one iota or shred of doubt. I have personally witnessed the manifestation of his holy power upon multiple occasions, just as I am experiencing it now. God is the ultimate arbiter and manifester of your destiny.

In fact, the words that are coming to my exact remembrance at this moment in time are the words of the Rev. Bishop T. D. Jakes. I have to tell you, as of this moment, it is a God thing.

I have not come clothed in the vesture of my past. Nor will I use the opinions of this world for my defense. No, I am far wiser through the things I have suffered. Therefore, I have come in my father's name. He has anointed my head, counseled my fears and taught me who I am: I am covered by his anointing, comforted by his presence and kept by his auspicious grace. Today, as never before, I stand in the identity He has given me and renounce every memory of who I was yesterday. I was called for such a time as this and I have come in my father's name.

Understand that most of the time, I am able to recognize God's imminent and masterful presence in my life. It is at that moment that I realize it is time for me to let go and let God work through me to say what he desires to say to the masses. I can feel the necessity to be obedient to the will of the Holy Spirit. He has something of great importance to say to you, and I can assure you that no matter how sinful you think your nature might be, God can still use and work through you as a means of achieving his ultimate purpose, bringing you closer to him for the total and complete salvation of your soul.

There is a deep, spiritually sagacious meaning in the phrase "It is more blessed to give than it is to receive." I don't mean that simply in terms of monetary compensation. God has allowed me to live long enough to watch every facet of this particular truth play out in my life. I've seen a lot of people die already and not understand the value of this great truth. It is indeed a sad commentary on the status of things in our lives when we become so attached to them that we can't part with them. God just did it again as I was writing this. Let me explain.

I'm not a minister, and I'm not good at reciting scripture. Yet as I pen this introduction at this moment, I go to retrieve my old worn-out, beaten Bible, and the scripture that keeps coming to my mind is Malachi 3:10. I check it, and lo and behold, I open it to the exact page, and my eyes fall immediately upon these words.

> Bring ye all the titles into the storehouse, that there may
> be meat in mine house and prove me now here with I will
> not open you the windows of heaven and pour you out a
> blessing that there shall not be room enough to receive.

I am most grateful that God has blessed me so abundantly. I am very thankful, and again, it's not just in terms of the monetary gain but in the deep, spiritual insights and wisdom that he has so graciously bestowed upon me. When God is at work in your life and takes the time to manifest himself to you and through you, there is absolutely nothing that anyone can do in your life that can prevent what God plans or wills for your life. The only thing others can ever do is look on with envy. And if they seek to do you harm, God will see to it that it is rectified as well.

So what possessions do you have that you can give that will illustrate to God you are serious about helping others? God looks to examine your heart to see whether you can truly value and trust his will for your life. I won't go into excessive detail, but outside of the Bible, I had in my possession a number of years back two of the most powerful books I had ever read on the art of success. Both were written in the 1800s. Needless to say, I thoroughly treasured those books.

The very last thing I had a desire to do was part with those books, and yet the Holy Spirit kept tugging at my heart to do just that. After a long and protracted battle with myself, I gave in to the Holy Spirit and parted company with two of my most insightful and treasured possessions: *Masters of the Situation: Some Secrets of Success and Power* and *The Royal Path of Life.* I was very selective of whom I chose to give those books. One went to my teaching colleague and personal friend Chad McKibben, and the other went to my lifetime friend Gene Murphy.

Little did I know at the time that a third book on success matters from that time period existed: *Pushing to the Front* by Orison Marden. This was one more example of how God works in such a miraculous manner to fill that empty void in your life, as evidenced in Malachi 3:10. The more you are able to trust and believe in God's profound truth for your life, the more he can do for you.

As Gene Murphy and I worked together, reading and immersing ourselves in these powerful, revealing books about successfully navigating through life, we coupled them with books written by the transcendentalists Emerson and Thoreau, as well as numerous modern-day success gurus like Tony Robbins, Zig Ziglar, Og Mandino, Les Brown, and John Maxwell. Recent passages that I read in Marden's book *Pushing to the Front* enabled me to fully understand the spiritual nature of what Gene and I had directly experienced. These are Marden's words.

> Two people with a strong affinity often call into activity a power in each other which neither dreamed he possessed before. Many an author owes his greatest book, his cleverest saying to a friend who has aroused in him latent powers which otherwise may have remained dormant.

> Artists have been touched by the power of inspiration through a masterpiece or by someone they happened to meet who saw in them what no one else had ever seen.

> The man who mixes with his fellows is ever on a voyage of discovery, finding new lands of power in himself which would have remained forever hidden but for association with others.

> Everybody he meets has some secret for him. If he can only extract it, something which he never knew before, something which will help enrich his life. No man finds himself alone. Others are his discoverers.

The Resolution of Perseverance

Making your mark on the world is hard. If it were easy, everybody would do it. But it's not. It takes patience, it takes commitment, and it comes with plenty of failure along the way. The real test is not whether you avoid this failure, because you won't. It's whether you let it harden or shame you into inaction, or whether you choose to learn from it; whether you choose to persevere.
—*Barack Obama*

The master who transcends the elements of those who choose to reside only in the common vernacular and adhere to the vulgar language of the common place appears only to those who acknowledge the benefits of metaphysical introspection. Excellence is characteristic of minds that seek the propensity of high thought and lingers not in the arena of befuddled mysteries.

As the great writer Gene Murphy once stated, "Time is the great orator of human achievement," and so time lends itself to the full consummation of integrity and honest means.

The quality that one must possess to reach the mark of the high calling resides in the armor of perseverance. A mind that will not bend to the structured mechanism of secularism will thwart the system that seeks to stymie it in order to proclaim the reverberations of nobility and truth.

Achievement is marked indelibly by a man's private manner and that which he claims in solitude will fully reflect his character in the open world. This is not philosophy but only that which is the greatest truth. The aberrations that incline themselves to fancy our folly must be released for the true master to reside as conqueror, because that which we seek is merely a reflection of our inner selves.

The maturation of eloquence and great thought comes with the pertinacious endeavors of self-discovery. When one has resolved himself to the sedulous enterprise of dismantling social chaos and injustice, it is then that he proclaims his freedom for the beneficence of man. When you lollygag with vermin and swine, it is your spirit that suffers through the deterioration of human carnality, because two forces are always at war within you. How is it that one child is miffed by circumstances and the other bends them to fit his will? It is character.

What tradition should one follow to realize his greatest ambitions, his greatest dreams? What should one do to tap his virtuous potential, to unleash his dormant energy that lies within his grasp? Is it the common traits of the English? What knowledge do these great people impart if they are to be studied with tenacity and keen observation? What would one learn? What truths have the great philosophers unearthed that remain hidden to 95 percent of the American populace today? It is this!

The human will is a mechanism designed to overpower any obstacle that attempts to confront it. Latin, Greek, and philosophy are the best medicines for the diets of young minds. High thoughts in the minds of youth will build character and lay the foundation for future generations. The problematic situations in the world cannot be remedied by the conceptual analysis of simplicity. That much is too obvious.

Men will not recognize truth. When they do, their foolish pride and arrogance will not allow them to accept it as truth. They are too busy going nowhere, trapped in the meaningless circle of ninety years they call life!

They live but do not learn; they hear but do not listen; they look but do not see. And their explanations are without merit. How can I tell them that I learned at thirty-six what Emerson knew at fifteen, but that most people will never learn in a lifetime? The measurement of credibility is evidenced by the centimeters of attitude. Accumulated wealth and positions of power are not always equivalent to character. Character cannot be bought or catered to, because character transcends the arena of metaphysics.

Life for man begins when he behooves himself to acknowledge his good and bad traits and seeks to fulfill his obligation to himself. Internal growth is the great benefactor of humanity; faith and temperament are the acquisitions of diligence and perseverance because these are the tools that produce results.

Results garner faith, heighten anticipation, and increase the avenues of hope. Through work, belief becomes the intercessor for the wanton prize. The fervor of the intellect feeds the mind with the air of expectancy.

Emerson said it best when he stated, "Nothing great was ever accomplished without enthusiasm." As the soul lingers under the spell of inspiration, the drunken stupor of exotic wisdom, and the captive influence of sagastic awareness, man comes of age. The perpetual youth of grown manhood is a quality of seeming rareness. It is invincible energy, this dedicated and untiring drive, that propels a man forward to meet his confrontations. Man's greatest adversary is himself. Because of his vexed adhesion to societal pressures, he believes himself to be far less than he actually is. Although potential and actuality bear the resemblance of brothers residing in similar cadres of endeavor, they are poised at opposing ends of the spectrum. The best good that deserves consideration knows no rest until the task is finished. The race of life will not barter incentive for a dole, and neither will it be encumbered by the subtle inconveniences of argument and frivolity. It answers only to undaunted perseveration.

It is this trait marked with the prerequisite of epistemology that augers well with the protuberance of power and place. To run with the grace and swiftness of the Asiatic gazelles, one cannot acquiesce to the orthodox style of common customs. Preparation and cunning are the weapons of the warrior, and the high resolve is the gift of the conqueror. For he who is drawn to attempt the veracity of human nature, let him understand that he must supersede the traits of commonality.

Opportunities do not guarantee the molding of the finished man; they must be met with the perfection of ability in an effort to usher in the brilliance of unity. Joint forces are the tenants of the highest persuasion and blend well with the aristocracy of elite thought.

It is well to note that the goals in life are not to be confused with the dreams. Goals are merely the avenues through which one must pass to obtain the elusive qualities of goodwill and harmony, for martyrs of justice, longevity, and quality are not common bonds. Martyrs seek truth, whereas the common man seeks toleration and mistakes existence for life.

The swashbuckling of Dumas and the military antics of Napoleon in the 1800s should prove for the modern thinker to be the highest role of emulation. If the discipline of execution is the example, the aspirations and accomplishments of these men surpass all levels of human understanding. Through a divine union with God, Jesus knew at age twelve the virtuous and exemplary power of humility, and he suffered man to transgress not against himself. While inconsistency hovers over the majority as the cloud of dark despair, bold intrepidation walks straight toward its goal. Resolutions of a trained mind fulfill the task of arduous thought and overshadow the indecisive mode of dissipating wishes. Wishes are nothing more than dreams of the derelict, fully unconscious of the advent of labor.

As fleeting smoke fills the sky to be dispensed in multiple directions by the mighty wind so that dreams devoid of action and lacking a fortress of consolidation dissipate into the chambered halls of desolation. Faith is the ardent lover of hard work and grows in eager anticipation with the exercising of right faculty. Work is the answer of the supplication of prayer and the vigorous challenge of future admonition.

Appearance is deceptive because the fruit of genius lingers on the verge of contemplation. High thought is the incubator for esteemed innovation. The high tower of life will not bow in serene fashion to the blowing winds of chance if the girders are anchored securely to the staunch stalwart of willful necessity. Thoughts are the mediators between God and men, and they must be guarded with the expectation of right manifestation.

To live fully is to understand the significance of total immersion geared toward the process of accomplishment. Desire for a life that is fulfilled needs no explanation. Was it not E. E. Channing who said, "Sometimes to dare is the highest wisdom"? It then falls upon the nature of nourishment to temper the pulse of right thinking in an effort to encourage excellence and instill character.

Quitting is worse than the resignation of death because in quitting, you must reside daily with the waking thoughts of doubt and fear. Death is the welcome liberator from a tormented hell and a stage of self-disclosure. The systematic design of apathy is the degrading spoiler of advanced learning, which fuses knowledge into a futile effort of docile emulation.

Continuity is the creator of unorthodox logic and self-teaching. But it is this kind of perseverance that fuels the logic of persuasion and draws the fiery dart with astounding and ebullient accuracy to the waiting bull's-eye. To fathom the sea of opposition is to render a solution designed for conquest. Life is filled with the adversaries of confrontation who would prefer the lot of humanity to remain in a menial disposition.

This knowledge alone should kindle a keen desire for innate growth and largess. A proclivity for the status quo is a boon to the lethargic mannerisms of tractability, but the vexations of foolhardiness will not be a temptress to the mode of solemn thought. A man becomes drunk under the ascertainment of liberated thought and sublimates his aims above those which are prevalent in the troubled masses. It is this exposition that frames the pattern of success. And what is success but the intangible dream of palpable substance ushered to verity by the complexity of resolution? Talent buys the dictator of possibility while genius sells the insurance policy of truth. Talent labors in the vineyard of the unsung while genius rests on the mountain of the sage.

The purity of thought is symbolic of God's original intent for man. It is this cause that elevates him to his rightful place in the great chain of being and harmonizes his goodwill with the spiritual sagacity of newness. It is then that the attributes of his reverent mind, under its complying to the acceptance of the Holy Spirit, seek out the answers to the conundrums of daily resurgence.

Faith is the supreme benefactor of sustentation and embodies the firm commitment of solidarity. As a great writer said, "The future success and happiness of an individual a family, a business, and a nation is built on faith. So long as this faith is strong, history shows that no trials are too hard to overcome, only when faith weakens then do people lose their ability to master their circumstance."

The greatest good of solemn thought is to master the art of self-governance. He who learns to govern himself holds the world in humble abeyance. The power of captivation is a by-product of the spoken truth. One man desires what another man has because of the admiration for character. It is foolish to desire for desire's sake. It is contemplation that will force the balance of proper action. The newness of life is granted through the unraveled mysteries of philosophic admirals. It is the generals of superior thought who plant the transitory seeds of renaissance.

The annoyance of commoners is misplaced; they would do better to acknowledge the misdemeanor of haughty pride. In the blind error of mischief, a chance for greatness is diminished.

The delicacies of virtue permeate the rose garden of life and nurture into full bloom the strength and texture of consistency. Effort is the artifice of manifold triumph and hedges in the heart of accomplished affairs. To work with the zealous fervor of an artist is no easy task, but it is the business of the man to learn the tools of the salient trade. When this is done, learning is hailed as a notable measure of growth while the application is viewed as the height of quintessence, or *sans peur et sans reproche*.

The indefatigability of perseverance is a noteworthy characteristic of higher achievers and becomes the modus operandi par excellence.

To draw upon confined knowledge is the error of grave reproach, because truth is the enlightenment of experienced culture. Transcend the apex of scholarship and cleave to the advancement of virtuous learning by acknowledging the spirit of neoteric fulfillment.

The level of subliminal intelligence is the exhilarating highway of the star galaxy that connects the virtuous qualities of freedom and independent thinking. To drink from the cup of open pages is to seek the highest truth of veneration.

When one has given his best, the nature of his accomplishment will stand on its own merit, and self-training will have served as the medicine for mental polarity and the structured course of willful thought. Dignity is often dressed in the apparel of sobriety and makes it imperative to avoid the path of blind folly. The antithesis of goodwill runs the parasitic gamut of devastation, which is marked as the high prize of Salem's lot, whereas procrastination defiles the veritable honor of complexity and cherished aims.

The inference of right action is the term given to dogmatic persistence. Staying the course is the key to the consecutiveness of successful ventures. Stopping is not the adversary; never starting sheds a light upon the closet skeleton of captivity. One does not do well to fit himself for a task of finite ventures. The aim of verity should rest within the complex realm of self-discovery. Intrinsic merit must become the forerunner of productive thought.

The mind is the instrument of preeminence and structures well the future course of human endeavor. It delicately molds the private aspects of fertile ground for public convolution and salvages only the best for fit consumers. What next is the augmentation of good logic mixed with the flavored recipe of creativity. This becomes the blissful guise of solid progression. The pressure of challenge is the harbored benefactor of prestigious orientation and the nucleus of perfect character.

The art of perception is the prose courier of erudition. It is wise for the learned thinker to acquiesce to the power of the subconscious will. It is this timely reserve that will dictate right action through the power of autosuggestion. The aggrandizement of full reconnaissance increases with the rule of supposition.

It is the war of substantive power and greed that presupposes intermission and advocates blatant denial for the honest earnings of working corollary. It would be well to mount the counterattack by virtue of a greater cause. Work with the present position and build a castle beyond the measures of grandiose proportion in the vector of the common reverie for what makes learning the substance of superior anticipation. He who is resolved in will may reign as the artistic champion of the working enterprise. The mode of simplicity is the welcome flight of opportunity. Many a good soul was cast out in the name of aspersion, only to return as the honored guest of veneration.

Listen closely to hear the barely audible sound of inspiration breathing the sweet, laureate lyrics of zephyr's repose. This concentration will mesh faith and action into the conjugal bliss of revered consummation. It is this approach that locks the door on the vulnerability of haughty arrogance and gives hot pursuit to the evaporating dreams of illimitable measure.

The beauty of decision lies within the nobility of smooth transition. Forward progress becomes the symbolic mark of dedicated perseverance.

Goals are the stepping stones to the palace of equanimity and the castle of the elegant rose. Their design is to the dream as the hurdle is to the race. With each step forward, the confronted challenge loses the face of adversarial conflict and in the end bows humbly before its master. Thinking is the evidence of superior intellect and applauds the contract of authoritative pursuit.

The opulent proclamation of driven commitment is an anchor on the raging sea of life. It is the stern countenance of determination that directs the creative flow of effulgent juices to the targets deemed the sources of the master.

Necessitation builds the admirable quality of cogent acumen and fills the mind with a deep-seated drive of conviction that compels the activated storehouse of knowledge to derive the appropriate solution for the natural bent. More often than not, the limitations of ability are merely the nature of unknowing self-impositions.

It is the chosen path of a selected few that surpasses the numerous callings of the many, and it is these few who will temper the direction of posterity. To develop an ardent love for character, one must fully learn himself. Ambition's corner is the mystique of grandeur and must be embraced in proper fashion, or else the sudden elevation in greatness will not equal the rapid fall.

To be great is to fully understand and comprehend the struggle of hardship. To be great is to understand the structure of human commitment. Above all, to be great is to acknowledge the temporal and ephemeral condition of humanity, and to know and value the fact that life is the precious commodity of grace.

Timidity is the quality of a loser's will and must be replaced with the persuasive air of confidence. The assertive tactic of known direction is the surety that sways the masses. The caliber of the man identifies itself by the nobility of his stature and the penetrating attributes of his desire. The proper position of authority is garnered, and followers work to either achieve or exceed the same level of mastery.

The mind's eye is the watchful agent for the advent of compending doom, and the soul is the guardian of salvation's testimony. Nothing can usurp the power of fruitage's moment, for when it falls upon the doorway of celestial fabric, it is cultivated in the mind as the prime harvest of the new blossom. Though one might wish to reach for the plateau of intuition, it falls by design to those obedient servants who exercise right thinking through the discipline of execution. Even with the morning's intrusion comes the call of the welcome God of industry.

The balance of temperament is the instruction of reason, and the prolific genre of past evidence bears a sufficient case for the sacred intervention of added spectacle in an effort to uproot the woeful chastisement of improper action. Under the guidance of wisdom, truth hails as the salient doctor of freedom and the selected finisher of compelling commitment. The nucleus of genius is the revealed commander of interception. The mind itself is the supreme determiner for the venture capitalist of generative enterprise.

One cannot dismantle the delicate dreams of dignity without confronting the dexterous challenge of bold and intrepid fate. The path of life has long adhered to the star of immortality. It is there for the explanation and vision's parable. The unanswered riddles of tomorrow's quest will become the open pages of today's journey with each approaching hour. It is only fitting to speak of time's challenge in molding receptive maturity. To wait is to understand fully the cherished quality of character and advanced patience.

A mind that is drenched in the temple of wisdom becomes the unique recipient of great honor clad in the virtuous apparel of goodwill, and it resolves to sequester the induced paradigm of indigenous purpose. It is this mind laden with the jewels of eminent wisdom that becomes the renewed vessel sustained for the soul's purpose of God's manifestation. The acute flourishing of Eve's ardor, which serves as the right order of truth, is founded on the stairwell of opportunity.

Verity becomes the filament of radiant light and seeks to placate the condescending diffusion of incalculable differences. It is the lamentation of weakness that is stilled by the delicate presence of candor and the resilient quality of fervent hope, which impregnates possibility for the purpose of high atonement. The ubiquitous message of honor's claim is the sweet nectar of Jupiter's revered approach amid the wellspring of good measure that is founded on the pedestal of tranquility.

The millennium of fortuitous thought acts as the great equivocator of impoverished expression to encourage the fellowship of distinguished savantry. One must relish the esoteric qualities of noble virtue and rest assured that the house of prudence guards against the derogatory avenue of ill conduct followed by the whisper of unduly deference, which displays the captive force of error's way. The embossed condition of stately character is the oracle of revolutionary insight that hails change as the imminent guardian of viable enhancement and the opulent classification of dignity. Work, then, is the price of admission to the harvest of plenitude, because labor will become the dictating intruder for the sake of prominent mastery. Then the watchdog of possibility will become the guardian for ambition's entree into the lineage of divine kings.

The expectancy of miracles adorned the entrance of the golden fleece, and in like manner it is the Trinitarian principle of divine concern that presupposes the uncommon traits of complex doctrine. This level of belief adheres to the emancipated concern of endowed genius. The perspicacious leverage of spiritual phenomena comes as a result of the meritorious reward of diligent seeking. It is this kind of faith that prompts the miniscule particles of cognition to affect the supreme constituent of the highest claims.

The challenges of daily confrontation are virtue's whetting stones for skillful living. To stay afloat amid the tumult of tempestuous failings is to demonstrate the adamantine courage of will. Will is the lifeblood of sustentation and the heartbeat that trudges upon the heel of each breath. When the will of the human spirit has obeyed its master and finished its course, it lays to rest the ultimate concern of continuous striving, and life becomes the silent repose of savored rest.

Until that approaching day comes to claim the tarrying soul as the host for salvation's army, let the words of the immortal sages make manifest to the deepest vein of your heart and the watchful soldiers who stand guard at the door of your mind.

> However brilliant, or however modest, may be one's ideal, the main thing after all, is to seek persistently its accomplishment; for however enchanting may be our castles in the air, they will prove of little real value unless we put foundations under them. Herein lies the great test of a man's power and ability. It is comparatively easy to form bright ideals but between the wish and the fulfilment the journey is often very long. Full many a soul has grown heartsick and weary by the way. All the heroic qualities in a man are thus put frequently to the severest test. The difference in man is nowhere more marked than right here. The persistency, the indomitable courage which brooks no defeat or the timidity which easily succumbs is then revealed. The high resolve and then death or victory is what brings success.

—William James Tilley

"Toil awhile—endure a while—believe always—and never turn back."

—Chinese Proverb

About the Author

Dr. Robert L. Lawson has amassed over thirty-seven years of experience serving as a teacher, administrator, adjunct professor, business entrepreneur, consultant, and writer. He began his educational career as an instructor at Gallia Academy High School and taught there in the field of English before moving on to Marshall University and serving as the director of continuing education for thirteen years. Shawnee State University came calling, and he served as the director of continuing education there for seven years before opening his own consulting firm to conduct empowerment training for eight years. He returned to the classroom at Georgetown Jr. Sr. High School and spent nine years there before taking his current position as an instructor of English for high school juniors and seniors at the request of then Principal Dr. Jeffrey Fisher at Chillicothe High School in Chillicothe, Ohio.

Dr. Lawson holds a bachelor's degree with a major in English and a minor in speech from the University of Rio Grande, a master's degree in English from Marshall University with a concentration in seventeenth-century literature, and a doctoral degree from Nova Southeastern University in the field of educational administration.

He has developed and taught numerous curriculums in the field of human potential, growth, and development, which includes such topics as how to stay motivated to win, maximizing your potential for greatness, changing your thinking, changing your life, how to make an effective presentation, becoming an effective leader, achieving excellence in the classroom, nuggets of wisdom, and daring to be a millionaire. In addition, he has co-authored *Oh Yes We Can! Black Achievement in America* with Gene Murphy, a publication that contains sixteen hundred questions and answers on the African American experience.

Books he has authored include *The Power of Optimism, The Triumph of the Spirit, Ageless Wisdom, The Gamer, Dare to Be a Millionaire, The Dare to Be a Millionaire Quotebook, What Every Teenager Needs to Know about Money, Piggy Bank Basics for Kids, Destined for Greatness*, and this long-awaited sequel to *Destined for Greatness, Greatness Awaits: Putting Your Dreams into Action*. *Destined for Greatness* was originally published in 1994, and so this sequel has been twenty-four years in the making. It contains the culmination of everything that Dr. Lawson has learned up to this point in time.

He is considered a scholar with tremendous expertise in the field of human potential development. Dr. Lawson is an outstanding presenter and professional speaker who mixes humor with wit, inspiration, and fact while leaving audiences both spellbound and empowered. He currently lives in Portsmouth, Ohio.

When he is not teaching or lecturing, he is giving empowerment presentations around the globe. His most requested keynote address is "Destined for Greatness." His e-mail address is rlawson68@hotmail.com, and his current mailing address is PO Box 2052, Portsmouth, Ohio 45662.